Time Travel in a Jeepney

A German-Philippine Journey Through Time

Originally published in German as

"Im Jeepney durch die Zeit"

FSC
www.fsc.org
MIX
Papier aus ver-
antwortungsvollen
Quellen
Paper from
responsible sources
FSC® C105338

For Mum and Dad

Content

Foreword

This book is our journey – a journey through time, through two cultures, two homelands, and two identities.

We, Christian (*1992) and Andrew (*1994), are brothers born and raised in Germany. But our roots reach deep into the Philippines. Our mother is Filipina, our father German – and from an early age, we lived between two worlds: between life in a Franconian village and tropical summers, between bratwurst and mangoes, between German village festivals and Filipino fiestas.

Germany and the Philippines differ in many ways – not only culturally, but also in geography, size, and population. The Philippines, located in Southeast Asia, consist of over 7,000 islands. Around 115 million people live there, across approximately 300,000 square kilometers. Germany, in Central Europe, is slightly larger at about 357,000 square kilometers but has a smaller population of roughly 84 million. The two countries are more than 10,000 kilometers apart – a distance reflected in their climates, daily lives, and worldviews.

Our story is shaped by these contrasts – by moments when we felt at home and others when we felt caught between worlds.

With this book, we invite you to join us on our personal journey through time. I, Christian, am writing these words, but my brother Andrew is with me every step of the way – this story belongs to both of us.

The jeepney, the iconic Filipino mode of transport, is more than just a way of getting around. It represents the Filipino spirit – colorful, full of stories, sometimes chaotic, but always full of life. That's exactly what our life between two cultures felt like. The title *"Time Travel in a Jeepney"* stands for our journey: a ride filled with memories, encounters, and experiences that shaped who we are.

Summers in the Philippines often felt like stepping into another time – a world where the clocks ticked more slowly, family came first, and life followed the rhythm of nature, festivities, and community.

Germany, on the other hand, was marked by structure, planning, and predictability. Two opposites? Maybe. But for us, it was always a balancing act – sometimes a bridge between two worlds, sometimes a stretch between them.

What can you expect from this book?

These are our memories, our experiences, and our reflections.

We share stories of festive nights in San Roque and cozy afternoons at village fairs in Franconia, of goodbyes and homecomings, of identity and belonging. It's about growing up in a globalized world, about migration, and about the question of how to live in two cultures without losing either one.

And sometimes, it's also about the search for treasure – about imagining that somewhere among the islands, there might still be gold, old maps, or forgotten stories waiting to be found.

But our story isn't unique. Maybe you'll recognize yourself in it, or maybe you know someone with a similar experience. Many people with migrant backgrounds navigate between two worlds – and it's these connections, challenges, and stories we want to share with this book.

Beyond that, we take a look at broader social topics – from migration to the cultural differences between Germany and the Philippines. We talk about the work of *Kinderhilfe Philippinen,* our personal experiences, and the themes we explore in our podcast *"Alman ist Lost."*

This book is our way of revisiting the moments that

shaped us – a ride in a jeepney that carries us not only through landscapes but through time itself. As different as our two homelands may be, they have both found a place within us – and have become one.

Hop on – and join us on this special journey.

PART 1: VIDEO TAPES (1996 - 2008)

Digitize

VHS tapes are like little time capsules for many families –
memories from an analog era, long before the digital age
began. Back then, special moments weren't captured on
smartphones or stored in the cloud, but on black plastic
cassettes, carefully labeled and stashed away in cabinets.
For years, they lay there unnoticed – patiently waiting to
be rediscovered.

For us, the real journey through time began in 2024,
when the idea for this book was born – and we finally
started digitizing all those old videos. With every image,
every sound, past moments came back to life – as if we
were traveling through time.

We borrowed an old VCR from my godmother (ours had
long since been thrown away), and after a short online
search, we found a suitable adapter to transfer the analog
recordings to our PC. It was the beginning of a massive
project: at least 50 tapes full of memories waited to be
brought back to life.

Our dad was an enthusiastic amateur filmmaker. With
his Super 8 video camera, he captured special moments –
including his visit to the 1972 Olympic Games in Munich.
Some of his earliest recordings were from trips to southern
France in 1974 and 1975, where he filmed places like St.
Tropez and Monaco. While capturing the impressive
landscapes and vibrant scenes, he narrated the footage
with his voice, telling little stories – precious memories
that might have been lost if we hadn't digitized the tapes
in time.

One story etched itself especially deeply into our
memory: his friend, who had been to France a few years

earlier, accompanied him on that trip. Together, they visited a French family he had stayed in contact with. The reunion was warm, almost familiar, and the shared meal was lovingly recorded by our dad. It was a journey into a past we never experienced ourselves – but which, through these tapes, suddenly felt close and vivid.

The footage also stirred feelings of longing and melancholy. How much we would have loved to watch these videos with him. But, as so often in life, things were postponed. Only after his death did we find the time – and the courage – to face these memories. We had to go through the footage alone, guess who the people in the recordings were, and try to imagine what these journeys must have been like for him.

The images from Monaco were particularly striking. Years later, at least one of us stood in Monaco – and recognized many things: the casino, the promenade, the exotic garden.

These tapes are more than just video material for us. They are a bridge to the past, a treasure that helps us preserve the stories of our family. Maybe we needed the time and maturity to take on this project. Maybe now was exactly the right moment to capture these memories – for us, for our family, and for everyone joining us through this book.

Before we arrive in the Philippines, the "check-in" comes first – and that includes not just our luggage, but also some important information about the country.

Chapter 1: Check-In

Preparing for our trips to the Philippines was its own little adventure every year.

Thanks to our mum, we were allowed a generous 40 kilos of checked baggage per person – a rule granted to families with Filipino roots, and one we took full advantage of each year. This special fare is called *Balikbayan,* which means "returning home." Those extra kilos were more than welcome – because we never traveled light.

Packing always started early – with a list that seemed to grow longer every summer. Alongside our own belongings, we often had items for friends or relatives who had asked us to bring a parcel or some specific product. These included gifts, special requests, or everyday goods from Germany that were hard to find over there. Our mum always made sure that nothing was forgotten.

Our own luggage was far from minimalist. The suitcases filled up with clothes for every occasion, German sweets, and little things we just couldn't leave behind. It was always a challenge to manage all those kilos, distribute them across the suitcases, and make sure none of them were overweight. Saying goodbye at the airport was always a balancing act – as we pushed our luggage and helped one another get everything to the check-in counter.

Every year, we told ourselves that next time, we'd pack less. But of course, with the growing excitement of going to the Philippines, the packing list grew too – and in the end, everything was once again packed right up to the last gram. All those kilos meant effort – but they also meant bringing a little piece of Germany with us. And that meant just as much to our family and friends there as it did to us.

Treasure Islands

The Philippines is made up of over 7,000 islands – a fascinating world full of stories, cultures, and mysteries. Many of these islands were already inhabited more than a thousand years ago, and that rich history is still reflected today in the country's diverse culture. Dances, music, languages, and traditions tell of a vibrant past shaped by ancient kingdoms, tribal societies, and bustling maritime trade.

Back then, Andrew, Dad, and I often wondered what treasures might be buried along the shores. Maybe we felt a bit like explorers as we dreamed of digging up an old chest somewhere – filled with gold, silver, or secret scrolls. But eventually, we had to accept the likely truth: someone had probably found that treasure long before we ever got there.

Maybe it was a treasure from the Spanish Armada. Or gold bars from the vault of a sunken U.S. military ship. Perhaps it was secret documents from an Arab trading vessel. Or even the legendary riches of a Japanese warship from World War II. Who knows – maybe something from the time of the Chinese seafarers, who sailed these waters long before the Europeans. One thing is certain: over the course of history, many have come here. Traders, conquerors, pirates, explorers – they all left their mark on these islands.

But one of the Philippines' greatest treasures is not made of metal or paper – it is nature itself. The breathtaking biodiversity, lush rainforests, vibrant coral reefs, and rare animal species are truly unique. Even though much of it was lost in the past, nature is slowly beginning to recover.

Today, many people are working to protect and restore these natural treasures – so they are not lost, but preserved for future generations.

Languages

The Philippines is incredibly rich in linguistic diversity. There are over 170 different languages and dialects spoken throughout the country – often completely different from one region to the next. The two most widely spoken languages are Tagalog, mainly used in and around Manila, and Visayan (also known as Cebuano), which dominates many southern parts of the country. Despite this linguistic variety, English is one of the country's two official languages – and for us, it was always the bridge to our family.

We never learned Tagalog or Visayan – even though the idea came up now and then. Instead, we stuck to English, which allowed us to communicate with our family in the Philippines without any trouble. For our mum, it was especially important back then to learn German quickly – not just for everyday life, but also to become independent, get a driver's license, and be able to work. Knowing the local language opens up entirely new possibilities for anyone starting out in a new country. And so, German became the language of our family life – and today, our mum speaks it impressively well and confidently.

Our dad had a much harder time. English was difficult for him because he had never learned it – it simply wasn't taught in school during his time. That lack of a foundation made things challenging, especially when interacting with our family in the Philippines. So when we traveled, we were almost constantly acting as translators. Someone would say something in Visayan, our mum would translate it into German for us, we'd speak to our cousins in English, and then translate everything back again for our dad – and so it went.

Sometimes we'd meet German friends along the way, and then the roles reversed: we'd translate from German into English for our Filipino family. It was a constant back-and-forth between languages – sometimes exhausting, but also kind of beautiful. A true coming-together through communication.

When we were back in Germany, we often missed all that translating and the linguistic diversity. In our little village in Franconia, you could of course get through daily life just fine with German. But as soon as we stood at the airport in Frankfurt again, surrounded by people speaking all kinds of different languages, it felt like a breath of fresh air. It was as if the world had come alive again – like we were finally back on the road.

Chapter 2: August 1996

We can hardly remember our very first flight – we were just under four and two years old at the time. Most of the memories live on today mainly through old photos, videos, and the stories our parents told us.

For our mum, this trip was a very special homecoming: for the first time in five years, she would set foot on Philippine soil again – but this time, not alone, but with the two of us by her side. It was also the first time we would meet our Filipino grandfather. We lovingly called him "Lolo Opa" – a mix of the Filipino word *Lolo* (grandfather) and the German *Opa*. Technically, it meant "Grandpa Grandpa" – a bit redundant, yes, but for us as little kids, it made things clear and easy to remember.

Everyone waiting for us in the Philippines was just as excited – aunts, uncles, cousins who had only ever heard about us in stories. A whole extended family, full of anticipation, eager to finally meet us in person.

It was also a big moment for our dad – because it was his very first flight ever. Even years later, he would tell us with a smile how nervous he had been back then. His first takeoff, his first time above the clouds – and all of that with two small children in tow. Plenty of adventurous stories came out of that trip: diapers that had to be changed mid-flight, getting lost in unfamiliar airports, and the juggling act of strollers, backpacks, and travel documents.

Over the years, the flights became almost routine. And like all things that are repeated, certain rituals began to form. At first, my brother and I sometimes sat apart, but soon we had our regular seats: usually in a two- or three-seat row by the window. Andrew traditionally got the window seat, I sat in the middle, and either Mom or Dad sat next to us. The other parent would usually sit just across the aisle – always close by.

Trips to the Philippines almost never happened without stopovers. Each year meant multiple layovers, discovering new airports, four flights total for the round trip – often with changing routes and different stopover cities. But all of that became part of the experience, part of the anticipation. The flights were more than just a way to get from one place to another – they became part of our family history. And perhaps even a quiet symbol of how we always made that journey together – connected, even across thousands of kilometers, somewhere between the sky and home.

While Dad and Andrew sat in the back, I sat in the front with Mum.

During our research, we came across an old photo that captured this special moment: Mum with the two of us, right after landing. Dad – as so often – was behind the camera, preserving that moment for us. A quiet reminder of a beginning we can no longer remember ourselves.

Of the few memories that have lasted to this day, one of them is my fourth birthday. I remember the birthday cake, the balloons – and how Andrew insisted on sitting right next to me at the cake.

Another memory takes me back to a trip to the island of Limasawa. It was a sunny day – a small journey of discovery on this historically significant island. Over the years, many more trips followed, each time with a growing family, and each time, this country became a little more familiar to us.

Even though the local language always remained foreign and we understood only a few words, our connection to the Philippines took deep root. This country will never feel unfamiliar – it is a home we are lucky enough to rediscover again and again.

San Roque, as beautiful as it gets – the beach of our childhood captured in a single image.

Jeepneys

Jeepneys are among the most iconic symbols of the Philippines.

Their origins go back to the period after World War II, when leftover U.S. military jeeps were transformed by Filipinos into colorful, creative shared taxis. The chassis was extended, benches were added – and with great attention to detail, these artistically decorated vehicles came to life. From the word "jeep" and the American term "jitney" (for shared taxi), the now-iconic "jeepney" was born.

Over the decades, jeepneys became not only a vital means of transportation but also a symbol of Filipino ingenuity and zest for life. Even amidst modern shopping malls, high-rises, and newly developed transport systems, they remain a familiar sight on the streets – colorful, loud, and full of character.

For us, every jeepney ride to the nearby city of Maasin was a little adventure. That's where we regularly did our shopping, ran errands, or visited relatives. There was no fixed schedule – you simply stood by the roadside and waited: sometimes ten minutes, sometimes thirty.

Boarding was always from the back – cramped, low, and far from comfortable. Vehicle inspections? Pretty much unheard of. But that was part of the charm. Everything felt a bit improvised, yet somehow, it all worked.

The driver would often stop along the way to refuel. Gasoline was sold roadside, bottled in old Coca-Cola bottles – one liter per bottle. Only as much fuel as necessary was bought, depending on the fare that had already been collected. It was a well-practiced system, where everyone knew their role.

The ride along the coastal road from San Roque to Maasin was always an experience. The breeze, the sound of the ocean, and the passing scenery created a sense of freedom, calm, and pure Philippine atmosphere.

These rides were simple – but special. They didn't just take us from point A to point B; they allowed us to experience the country, its people, and everyday life up close. Even though much has changed over the years, the jeepney remains at the heart of that experience – a rolling piece of home and memory.

Fiesta

Every year during the second week of August, the fiesta began in our Philippine hometown – a village celebration that brought together the entire community, along with many former residents from all over the world. Since the festivities coincided perfectly with the Bavarian summer holidays, we were able to be there for the fiesta many years in a row. This week, full of rituals and traditions, had become very dear to us.

The celebrations began days before the actual feast day on August 16. The program was colorful and varied, featuring bingo nights, dance and talent competitions, and concerts by live bands that created a festive atmosphere and got people dancing. Sometimes there were even small theater performances. We were often there right at 8 PM, ready for the show to begin – but in true Filipino fashion, things rarely started before 10. As German as we sometimes were, party was party – and eventually, we got used to it and simply enjoyed the atmosphere until things really kicked off.

On August 16th itself – the highlight of the fiesta – we celebrated not only Saint Roque but also my birthday. It became a tradition for me to attend the early morning mass at 6 AM with Mum, my aunt, and my uncle. Andrew and Dad would sleep in and join us later for breakfast. In the afternoon, the big parade took place: all the school classes marched in their uniforms, each with its own instruments. Music and laughter filled the village, and the parade ended at the school, where every class performed on stage.

The fiesta was always a reunion, too. Many family

members came back home – those who lived abroad or worked on ships. Not everyone could make it every year, but for those who did, it felt like truly coming home. That's how it was back then – and that's how it still is today.

Aliens

As children, the Philippines was a land full of mysteries and stories – a place where the line between reality and imagination often seemed to blur. One of those stories was about the "aliens at the waterfall." The waterfall lay just outside the village, hidden behind thick greenery. We rarely went there, but every time it was mentioned, that old tale would immediately come to life again – vivid in our minds.

It wasn't a story people talked about much. But now and then, someone in the village would casually say something like, "They say there's something up by the waterfall." Whether they really meant aliens or just strange beings – perhaps spirits or people from another world – was never entirely clear.

Stories like that are simply part of life in the Philippines. Alongside the widespread Christian faith – especially Catholicism – and Islam in the southern regions, there are still many ancient, nature-based beliefs. These include the idea that spirits and beings dwell in rivers, trees, mountains, or waterfalls. Such old beliefs often exist quietly alongside formal religion – naturally, and without contradiction.

Maybe our "aliens" were really nature spirits – or just a product of our childhood imagination. But that's what made the story so special: it was never frightening, never fully real, yet all the more fascinating because of that. A small mystery in the middle of everyday life, one that filled our childhood in the Philippines with a sense of magic and wonder – in a country where faith, superstition, and storytelling have always gone hand in hand.

Chapter 3: Christmas 1997

In our childhood, we almost always traveled to the Philippines during the Bavarian summer holidays – but that wasn't the case in the early years. Back then, we could still take advantage of cheaper flights outside the holiday season. That's how, in December 1997, we set off on a very special journey: Christmas and New Year in the Philippines. For the next 21 years, it would remain our only Christmas there.

We spent the holidays under palm trees, far from the cold winter months in Germany, without our grandma and the rest of the family back home. It was something new – and special in many ways.

Some fragments from that time have stayed with me. For example, the artificial Christmas tree we decorated with chocolate ornaments – an idea that didn't last long. In the tropical heat, the chocolate quickly melted, creating a sweet, sticky surprise. Strangely, we had already bought our presents in a supermarket in Cebu before Christmas Eve. That confirmed what I had already suspected for a while: the *Christkind* or Santa Claus didn't seem to have much to do with these gifts.

The Christmas celebration with the Filipino side of the family was a feast of its own. We sat together, laughed, and ate – a traditional holiday meal, but quite different from what we knew in Germany. The table was far too small for all the relatives – but no one seemed to mind. The celebration kept growing; more and more people came and went, and voices filled the night air. It was Christmas in a different way – a celebration full of joy and warmth, despite the heat that lingered even into the night.

At that time, Philippine Airlines still flew directly from Frankfurt to Manila – something that would no longer be possible in the years that followed. In many ways, that trip was unique: the direct flights, Christmas far from home, and the feeling of escaping the German winter for a short while to celebrate the New Year in the sun.

It would take 21 years before we spent Christmas together again in the Philippines. One last time as the four of us. One last time sharing those memories – a tradition and a farewell all at once.

The two of us with our dad in our grandpa's bamboo hut.

* * *

Christmas lights in San Roque: Impressions from 2018.

Well

As children, it was part of our daily routine to fetch water from the well.
The well was about a ten-minute walk away, and we would stand there with our older cousins, pump the water, and carry it back home.

Tap water wasn't necessarily safe to drink – and we knew that. Buying bottled water was an extra expense that not everyone could afford. So for us, it was completely normal to get our water from the well. While this routine felt unusual at first – especially for kids used to drinking straight from the tap in Germany – it was simply part of life in the Philippines.

In those moments, as we carried bucket after bucket of water home, we began to understand the value of something we had always taken for granted. Here, water was more than just a resource – it was a daily necessity that required effort and wasn't to be wasted.

Looking back, it's one of those memories that taught us a small but important lesson for life.

Cockfighting

In the Philippines, cockfighting is more than just a game – it's almost a sacred affair. For our grandfather, too, this tradition held a special significance. He was proud of his rooster, which he trained and cared for diligently. I can't quite remember how many fights his rooster actually won, but one thing was certain: it lived a long life – which suggested it hadn't lost many.

Most cockfights end in bloodshed, often in death. Gambling is inseparably linked to these fights. People from all walks of life gather in hopes of striking it lucky with a bet. The atmosphere in the arena is electric with tension as the fighting roosters face off. Equipped with sharp blades attached to their legs, they lunge at each other under the captivated gaze of the crowd.

Perhaps one day, time will catch up with this tradition —but in the Philippines, change often takes longer to reach the islands. Cockfighting is certainly no longer in step with modern values, that much is clear. Yet it remains deeply rooted in Filipino culture, and so it's uncertain if or when this aspect of daily life will truly change.

Until then, cockfighting continues to be a tradition that brings people together —for better or for worse.

Lottery

Every Wednesday and Saturday, it was the same ritual: our dad played the lottery. It was a small, deeply rooted routine in his daily life. In the Philippines, this ritual became a special challenge because the time difference meant the draws there always took place on Thursday and Sunday mornings. But that never stopped our dad from getting the lottery numbers – it was simply part of his routine.

In the earlier years, when there were no cell phones or internet, our dad often had to walk to the next village to use a phone booth to find out the winning numbers. On those Thursdays and Sundays, he would call our grandma, and she would already have the numbers ready. Before she told him the results, she always asked how we were doing in the Philippines – as if the number ritual was also a chance to check in and hear how the vacation was going. She wanted to know if everything was okay, how the weather was, and what we had been up to. That was typical for our grandma – the lottery was just a side story; the family connection always came first.

"How are you, is everything okay?" she would ask each time before reading out the numbers. While we answered, our dad would already be sitting next to us, pen in hand, ready to write them down. As soon as she gave him the numbers, she would pause for a moment and then add, "So, any luck?" Most of the time, of course, we didn't have the right numbers – but that didn't really matter. Somehow, this little ritual became a permanent fixture in our lives.

Later, as technology advanced and we finally had cell

reception on the hill near our village, the ritual changed a little. Dad often went up the steep path on his own to check the numbers directly by phone – no more phone booth needed.

Once, shortly before we were due to fly back to Germany, a situation came up that made our dad truly nervous. We were supposed to fly back on a Saturday, but due to delays, we didn't arrive in Germany until Sunday afternoon. He hadn't submitted the lottery ticket for that Saturday, thinking we would be back in time. "Imagine if those were the winning numbers this time – and the ticket doesn't count," he said seriously. For a moment, the thought of a missed jackpot really seemed to trouble him.

When we finally arrived in Germany on Sunday afternoon and checked the numbers, it turned out – luckily – that they were the wrong ones. What a relief. The idea that the big win might have come on that Saturday would probably have haunted us for a long time.

There was also a lottery in the Philippines – and just like in Germany, we often saw people standing in front of small booths, hoping for a big win. The longing for a shortcut to a better life seemed to be the same everywhere. But alongside the official lotteries, there were also many other, less legal gambling options, where wages were often gambled away in advance. Despite the risks, the hope for an unexpected windfall kept many people trying again and again.

In the end, we never won the big millions, and the dream of early retirement remained unfulfilled. But this ritual – whether it took place in a phone booth in the neighboring village, with our grandma on the line, or on the hill with poor reception – was more than just a habit. It was a small but constant connection between us, Germany, and the Philippines – a mix of hope, family closeness, and the joy of the game.

Chapter 4: February 1999

In February 1999, we took our last trip to the Philippines before I started school. We took the opportunity, knowing that from that year on, we would be bound to the summer holidays and could only travel during the German summer months. This trip fell during one of the most beautiful times of the year in the Philippines – it was pleasantly warm without the oppressive heat that often comes later in the year. The typhoon season was over, so we were able to fully enjoy island life.

Many memories from that trip have faded – as is often the case with our earliest years – but one scene after our return has stayed with me to this day. We had brought back mangoes and sweets from the Philippines, enough to share with all our friends at kindergarten. And so, after the vacation, we returned to kindergarten with a small suitcase full of exotic treats. The mangoes caused great excitement – and we had a cheerful little "welcome back" party.

This final trip before starting school marked the end of a free, flexible time when we could travel whenever it suited us and our parents best. Soon, school would shape our yearly rhythm, and our travels would always fall during summer break. But the memories of that February – of the warm sun and the joy in kindergarten – remain the perfect ending to those early travel years.

Peso Millionaire

One thing we kept encountering in the Philippines was the casual handling of numbers – especially when it came to the term "millionaire." We often heard about someone our dad always referred to as the "peso millionaire." The title had a certain ring to it – almost something respectful – and as children, we didn't quite understand what it meant, but the phrase stuck with us. "Peso millionaire" – it sounded impressive. Over time, though, we came to realize that the title didn't necessarily mean the same thing it would in Germany.

The exchange rate of the peso fluctuated greatly over the years. Sometimes the peso was strong, sometimes weak, and the rates moved within a wide range. At the time I was writing this chapter, the exchange rate was 1 euro = 62 Philippine pesos (as of October 24, 2024). With that in mind, we realized that becoming a "millionaire" in the Philippines theoretically wasn't all that difficult – even without winning the lottery. All it would take was about €15,960.76 – a sum that may seem large, but certainly doesn't scream luxury by German standards.

Still, one thing is clear: the peso millionaire – who often sponsored local events and was happy to help when the church roof needed fixing – was by no means poor.

World Receiver

Our dad was someone who could easily get excited about technology. One day, he came home with what was called a "world receiver" – a radio that was supposed to have good reception anywhere in the world.

"Does that really work?" we wondered.

He had been talked into buying the radio in Germany, convinced it would add a little connection to home during our summer adventure in the Philippines. The idea of listening to German radio while in faraway Asia was an appealing thought to him.

As soon as we arrived in the Philippines, the world receiver was unpacked and placed on the veranda. There, our dad would sit almost every morning, holding the small device in his hands, eyes fixed on the frequency display as he searched patiently. It seemed like he would spend hours tuning across the range – hunting for familiar sounds from Germany. But no matter how much he turned the dial and searched, he never really succeeded.

Once, he picked up a Japanese station, which surprised us all. Another time, he caught a Korean broadcast. The voices sounded unfamiliar, and we had no idea what was being said – but for a moment, our dad was still content: at least he had found something exotic. On another day, he stumbled upon an American military station broadcasting from a nearby base. The military music and brief English news reports caught his attention – but it wasn't what he was looking for.

Of course, there were also Filipino stations, constantly playing loud music and cheerful chatter – but that wasn't what he wanted either.

Our dad remained persistent – the same routine every morning. He extended the antenna with a copper wire and sat on our veranda, listening to the crackling, static-filled frequencies, turning the dial again and again – holding on to the quiet hope that one day he might catch a German radio station. But week after week went by, and we heard everything except German radio. Not a single European signal ever made it through.

In the end, the world receiver became more of a nostalgic object than a working device. He had hoped it would bring a bit of German homeland to our veranda – but in the end, the reception remained as distant as home itself. Instead, we heard the voices of the world – Japan, Korea, America – but German radio remained an unfulfilled wish.

Backpacker

Some memories stay with you forever – and this is definitely one of them. I was around eight years old, and although it was only a brief encounter, it left a deep impression on me.

A young German backpacker had come to visit. We had met him the day before at a small restaurant with a dive shop. Our dad, always open and curious toward strangers, had spontaneously invited him – and sure enough, he showed up the next day.

He was probably in his early twenties, maybe no older than 22, and told us he was traveling alone through the Philippines. The decision to go on the trip had been completely spontaneous, he said. He had come across a cheap flight somewhere and thought, "Why not?" Without a concrete plan, he simply let himself drift. At some point, a bus had brought him to Leyte – and when he saw the landscape, he decided to stay. "It's nice here," he said casually, as if already thinking about the next place.

The lightness with which he traveled – that sense of unbound freedom – left a lasting impression on me. Backpackers did occasionally pass through the Philippines, but our area was remote and rarely on their route. That's probably why this encounter stayed with me so vividly.

I still remember how I listened to him as he talked about his adventures. It was fascinating to meet someone who moved so freely through the world – with no fixed destination, just a desire to explore.

Even though it was only a short moment, it stayed with me over the years. Maybe it was this encounter that first sparked my wanderlust – the desire to one day set off myself, to see new places, to discover the world with my own eyes.

Chapter 5: Summer Vacation 2000

In the summer of 2000, we spent the school holidays in the Philippines for the first time – and decided to build a house in our second home. Many German-Filipino families take this step, and it connects us with so many others who have found a second home far from Germany. Building a house for the family was more than just a project – it was a kind of anchor, something that strengthened the bond to our mother's homeland.

The desire to create a home in a family's country of origin is not a uniquely Filipino phenomenon. We encounter it time and again – among friends with all kinds of migration backgrounds. Whether from Kosovo, Turkey, Pakistan, Thailand, or other parts of the world, many of them tell similar stories. Building a house, buying an apartment, having a permanent place for the family – this need is something that unites us.

I'm convinced: anyone with friends whose roots lie abroad will have heard stories like these too.

Departure mood: The four of us at Frankfurt Airport, 2000

House Construction

It was a major project that would shape our lives in the Philippines forever. The construction of our house began with a simple but crucial step: palm trees had to be cut down. These were used as makeshift scaffolding and helped establish the first structures of the house. In a photo from that time, my brother and I are standing as children in front of the unfinished building – an image that still keeps the memories of those days alive.

The construction took about a year. It was more than just a building – it was a home for our family, especially for our grandfather, who lived there and found a permanent place in this new house. From the very beginning, it was built to offer him a comfortable life and to serve as a gathering place for the whole family.

Our dad, a passionate handyman, found great joy in the project. For him, building the house was more than just work – it was a labor of love. He wasn't just constructing a home; he was creating memories, stability, and a sense of belonging that has stayed with us to this day. Every day was marked by sweat, strength, and the tireless drive to build something lasting.

Today, the house still stands. It has weathered the years – countless rainy seasons, storms, and sunny days. But one thing worries us: the shoreline. Every year, the beach creeps closer. Rising sea levels and natural shifts in the coastline leave us concerned. How long will the house remain safe? How long will it withstand the sea?

But as long as it stands, it remains a symbol of what our parents created – a home for our family, a place full of memories, and a piece of our second home that connects us to the Philippines.

Early construction phase – Andrew on the left, me on the right, together in front of the unfinished house.

Rice

We were eight and six years old when we sat in a local fast-food restaurant in the Philippines. Outside the entrance, we noticed a beggar who had no legs. He was sitting on a small board with wheels – right in the middle of the busy hustle and bustle. People passed by him – businesspeople, vendors, families – and yet hardly anyone seemed to notice him. To many, he was simply part of the everyday cityscape.

But we had seen him, and his presence stayed with us. In the days before, we had already noticed that a few people who could afford it would sometimes bring him something to eat. As we stood at the counter, Andrew decided to order a serving of rice – not for himself, but for this man. We gave it to him, and the expression on his face was unforgettable: a brief moment of gratitude and joy, a spark of hope.

At the time, we didn't fully understand the gravity of what we had witnessed. But over time, we came to realize how common it was in the Philippines to see people like him living on the streets. And yet, it's anything but normal. In a world of abundance, where many eat too much while others barely have enough, inequality becomes starkly visible.

Much has improved in the Philippines over the past decades – that's undeniable. But poverty hasn't disappeared. There are still people living below the poverty line, without real hope for change. They are the invisible victims of a system that doesn't work for everyone.

That encounter left a mark on us. It reminds us how

important compassion and humanity are. It may have been just a small act – a portion of rice – but in that moment, it might have meant everything to someone.

That's why we want to highlight the work of *Kinderhilfe Philippinen*, an organization that supports disadvantaged children and families. In Chapter 24, you'll learn more about how this organization brings hope and perspective. It's one way to take action – because no one should be overlooked in a world full of abundance.

Free Flights

However, on the journey home via Manila, there was an unexpected twist. Our flight from Cebu was delayed, and unfortunately, we missed our connecting flight in Manila. Our tickets had already been given away – the standby list in Manila is long, with many people hoping for spontaneous connections, such as flights to Dubai. As a result, our seats were assigned to other passengers, and we had to stay in Manila.

Fortunately, the airline was extremely accommodating and arranged an overnight stay for us in a hotel. In addition, we each received a free flight for the following year as compensation – a gesture that more than made up for the inconvenience.

It would be another 18 years before we experienced such luck again.

The two of us at the Waterfront Hotel, Cebu City – in the year 2000.

Together in Manila – Andrew, Dad, and me. It would be 18 years before we returned to the same hotel again.

Chapter 6: Summer Vacation 2001

In the summer of 2001, we were able to stay in our own house in the Philippines for the first time. The trip was planned quickly, since we still had the free tickets from the airline and were able to organize our stay earlier than usual. Preparations were in full swing – the 40-kilo baggage allowance per person wasn't enough, so we sent several packages ahead of time to have everything we needed ready. Our dad, a passionate handyman, of course brought his tools. There was hardly a day without hammering, sawing, or building going on somewhere – he always found something to do or improve.

The house was still simply furnished at the time – there was no TV and no modern distractions. So we often spent the long, warm evenings playing board games and doing puzzles. We would sit together for hours, and time seemed to pass more slowly – without news, without interruptions.

Before the trip, we had bought a few CDs that would become the soundtrack of that summer. *Best of 2001* left a lasting impression. Songs like "Whole Again" by Atomic Kitten or "Miss California" by Dante Thomas played – like all the other tracks on the CD – on repeat. Even today, when we hear those songs, we think back to those relaxed moments, playing games or puzzling together, shutting the world out.

That summer also, as so often, coincided with the Fiesta. It was tradition for our grandpa to come by with his band to kick off the festivities at our house. A regular part of the band was "Trumpet Grandpa" – a relative around our grandpa's age who, as the name suggests, played the trumpet. The band came every year during Fiesta Week and performed on our veranda. The atmosphere was joyful, the whole family came together, and music filled the house and garden. Our mum filmed it all for our home video collection, so we could always relive those summers. Moments like these made the summers in our second home especially beautiful.

This time, the journey home went according to plan – no delays and no free flight. The Fiesta in San Roque became our regular gathering point, and it turned out that we saw most of the family there. Visiting everyone in different places became increasingly difficult over time – so the festival became a meeting place and a welcome reason to spend time with (almost) the entire family and feel at home again in our second homeland.

Furnish

A house only truly becomes a home once it's furnished. After building the house, the next big step was setting it up. Many things were bought locally, but some items that would make the house feel more complete were sent from Germany. The kitchen cabinets were especially important – we shipped them to the Philippines in a container. It was an unusual choice, but for us, it made sense, as it was difficult to find comparable cabinets locally.

When the container finally arrived, it was an event in itself. The cabinets were unloaded and installed right away. It felt a little strange at first to see German furniture in a house in the Philippines – as if a piece of our first home had blended with our second. The kitchen was finally complete, and with it, a small piece of everyday life returned.

But a house is more than just four walls and a roof – it also needs to be blessed. In the Philippines, this is done through a traditional blessing ceremony. A local priest came to bless our house and pray for protection and good fortune.

At the heart of the celebration was the Santo Niño, one of the most important religious figures in the Philippines. A small statue of the Holy Child was placed on a decorated altar, and during the ceremony, prayers were said, holy water was sprinkled, and candles were lit. The atmosphere was festive – and after the blessing, as tradition requires, there was a shared meal with family, friends, and neighbors.

With this celebration, our house became more than just a building – it became a home. A place where tradition and

modern life, Germany and the Philippines, family and
community all came together.

46

Great-Grandfather

Our grandpa became a great-grandfather, and with the birth of our cousin's son, we gained a new playmate who would be part of our lives for years to come. It brought a new dynamic to the family – suddenly, we were no longer the youngest ones, but those stepping into the role of older relatives and role models.

Our little second cousin grew up alongside us. He wore our old clothes – the ones we had only outgrown a few years earlier.

But it wasn't just us who looked after him. As is common in many Filipino families, caring for him was a shared responsibility. Everyone took part in raising him: our aunts, uncles, cousins – all kept an eye on him and made sure he grew up safe and loved.

Two years later, his little sister was born – and once again, the family dynamic shifted. Suddenly, he was the older brother, and we watched as he began to take on responsibility himself – just as we had done with him.

The years passed, and the little children who once followed in our footsteps became independent individuals with dreams and paths of their own. But that time, when we all grew up together, remains one of the most cherished memories we associate with our second home.

Andrew together with the two of them – 2008.

Puzzle

In the first year we moved into our house in the Philippines, everything was still very different. We had no television, no internet, no smartphones to distract us. So we spent our time doing things that truly brought us together: we did puzzles, played board games and cards. It was a time when we simply lived in the moment.

There wasn't much else to do but listen to music or read – and that was a good thing. We had brought enough books, and instead of jumping from one notification to the next or endlessly scrolling through feeds (which in 2001 wasn't even possible yet), we immersed ourselves in stories or spent entire afternoons slowly completing a puzzle, piece by piece. No constantly flashing screens, no overwhelming stream of news demanding our attention – just the sound of the ocean, the chirping of crickets, and the voices of our family around us.

We often didn't even know what day of the week it was – and it didn't matter. We lived with the sun, waking with it and going to bed when it set. We collected seashells on the beach, bought fresh mangoes at the market, and let ourselves drift without thinking about tomorrow. The days were unhurried – and so were we.

Sometimes, I miss that early time without distractions: the endless hours we spent simply sitting together and playing; the calm that settled over the days; the simplicity that allowed us to truly enjoy the moment. It was a different world – a different time. And maybe that's exactly what made it so special.

Chapter 7: Summer Vacation 2002

In 2002, our travel route changed: for the first time, we flew via Hong Kong directly to Cebu, skipping Manila. This saved us a domestic flight and got us to our island, Leyte, much faster.

In the background, the *Best of 2002* CD with Enrique Iglesias was playing, and the younger family members danced joyfully to the music. When we watch the old VHS tapes today, we immediately feel the carefree happiness of that time again.

We even started building a ping-pong table out of palm wood. We had gotten the exact measurements from our local sports club back home – and then got to work. The tabletop was cut, assembled, and finally painted green. It was a true team project that tested not only our enthusiasm for sports but also our do-it-yourself skills.

For the first time, we also held a video camera ourselves and filmed our own experiences. The results were far from professional, but that didn't matter – it was fun, and we captured many small moments that still stay with us today.

The summer of 2002 was a time of change – of small and big projects, and of carefree family life. It was a summer in which things slowly began to shift, even if we didn't quite realize it at the time. But looking back now, we know: it was a time we'll never forget.

Andrew at the ping-pong table, focused and ready for the return shot. The net – improvised and clamped in place with screw clamps.

TV

A first that summer: for the first time, we had a television in the house. Until then, we had spent our time doing puzzles, playing board games, or simply having long conversations on the veranda.

One vague TV memory from our childhood has stayed with us to this day. It was a Filipino series that aired around 7 p.m. – something about a cavewoman with a broken heart, or something along those lines. Of course, we barely understood what it was about back then, but somehow we kept watching anyway.

Over time, Filipino television changed as well. While we had once received only a few local stations, a whole range of cable channels eventually became available, and the programming grew more diverse. Even *Deutsche Welle* suddenly appeared. Although the channel broadcast worldwide and often repeated its content, it was still nice to see something German in the Philippines – and to feel, at least sometimes, that Germany wasn't so far away after all.

The new channels brought further changes. A talent show for kids that we knew from Germany was now also being aired in the Philippines. It was a special feeling to visit relatives and see the same show on their screen that was also playing back home. Back then, television was a little window to the world for us – but also a piece of German life that was gradually becoming part of our everyday life in the Philippines.

Yet with all the new possibilities television offered, we sometimes wondered whether it was really an improvement. In the past, when the power went out and

we sat by candlelight, the time we spent together was
often just as beautiful. We would sit together, do puzzles,
read, or tell stories – simple moments that gave our days a
gentle rhythm. The world felt smaller – and sometimes, a
little more peaceful.

Football

In the summer of 2002, the FIFA World Cup in Japan and South Korea had just come to an end, and we had cheered for Germany – right up until they lost to Brazil in the final. Despite the bitter defeat, in which "Titan" Oliver Kahn made a crucial mistake, we still celebrated the national team's performance.

Amid all the excitement, we began to wonder whether the Philippines had a national team too – and in fact, they did. However, back then, it wasn't particularly successful.

That has since changed: today, the Philippine men's team plays at a solid level, even if qualifying for the World Cup still seems far off. The women's team, on the other hand, has already made a name for itself and even managed to score a victory against New Zealand at the 2023 World Cup.

What both teams have in common is the diversity of their players. Many have roots in Germany, the United States, Australia, or Canada. The Philippine Football Federation actively embraces this diversity, scouting worldwide for talents who want to play for their second home.

Lustige Taschenbücher

The *Lustige Taschenbücher* (a popular German comic book series featuring Donald Duck and other Disney characters), or LTBs for short, were a fixed ritual for us as kids – an essential part of our summers in the Philippines. Over the years, we built up quite a large collection and still remember that, back then, each LTB cost only 3 German Marks and 95 Pfennigs – they're much more expensive today. Still, they remained something special, and every year before our trip, we picked out a selection for the journey. Each of us was allowed to choose five or six books, so we ended up taking around twelve with us – twelve books full of adventures that would accompany us through five to six weeks of summer.

It became a familiar routine: as soon as one of us finished a book, it went straight to the other. The stories were shared, the adventures discussed and revisited again and again. For us, it was a time when we brought the heroes from Duckburg on every trip. Donald Duck, in particular, stood out – a loyal companion during our summer holidays.

Looking back, we regret that we eventually stopped reading the LTBs. The collection is no longer complete, and sometimes, when we spot one in a shop today, a wave of nostalgia washes over us. It's tempting to start again and continue the collection. Maybe one day, the time will come – and the adventures of Donald and friends will find their way back into our lives.

Weddings

Weddings in the Philippines are celebrated in many different ways – depending on the couple's and their families' budget, they can be lavish or simple. From extravagant beach ceremonies with family flying in from around the world to budget-friendly mass weddings held in church, every variation can be found.

For many couples, the church ceremony is a must – even if that means being married alongside several other couples in a joint service to save on costs. The reception itself may remain modest, but the significance of the church blessing is central for most.

Larger weddings, on the other hand, spare no effort: cinematic intros portray the couple as the stars of a romantic drama, professional beach photos are taken by the bonfire, and the celebration becomes a cultural highlight for the entire family. These weddings often serve as major family reunions – with relatives traveling from far and wide, sometimes even from different continents.

After the wedding, however, there is often little time left for a honeymoon. For many, the next step is heading abroad – often to work in the cruise industry or hospitality sector – to support the new family financially. Eight months at sea is not uncommon.

Still, the wedding celebration in the Philippines remains unforgettable: a joyful and proud moment shared by the bride and groom with their family and community.

Chapter 8: Summer Vacation 2003

In the summer of 2003, we felt for the first time what loss truly means. Over Christmas, our grandma had passed away in Germany, and it was our first real encounter with the finiteness of life. She had always been a constant part of our daily lives, living just one floor below us – together with her partner, who had become like a substitute grandfather to us. Our biological grandfather had died before we were born.

But 2003 brought more than just personal farewells – it was also the year of the SARS pandemic, which was spreading across Asia and causing concern. Even before our departure, friends and acquaintances asked whether we really intended to travel to the Philippines. We had thought about it, but according to the German Foreign Office, the situation seemed safe. In hindsight, we were fortunate that the pandemic never reached the scale of COVID-19, which would go on to drastically change the world 17 years later. Still, for the first time, we became aware of the global risks of pandemics – and that it wasn't so unlikely for an outbreak to one day make travel impossible.

In Hong Kong, where we had our layover, we clearly felt the impact of the pandemic: temperature checks were carried out everywhere, and hygiene notices were posted at every entrance and on every screen. It was strange to walk through a city where you could feel that an invisible threat hung in the air.

When we arrived in the Philippines, it was still a familiar summer – the first one without our grandma, but still a time of many changes. By then, we had TV reception and were able to follow the news and lottery numbers via *Deutsche Welle*. Even better for both of us was that we could now keep track of how our favorite football club, 1. FC Nürnberg, was doing – home felt a little closer, even on the other side of the world.

Our cousins were getting older; some were already in college and no longer around all the time. The Fiesta remained the highlight of the summer and gradually became one of the few moments when we saw almost the entire family together. Little by little, life began to pull us in different directions – and summer in the Philippines took on a new meaning. It became a time of reunion, growing more precious as the opportunities became fewer.

Jollibee

Every time we took the jeepney from our village, San Roque, into the city of Maasin, it felt like a little adventure for us as kids. A ride cost around 25 pesos back then. In Maasin, the nearest city, more and more shops were popping up—larger and more modern than before. And then, in the mid-2000s, something happened that was a huge deal for us brothers: a Jollibee opened. To us, it felt like a little paradise. Jollibee was the Filipino version of McDonald's—but it was more than that. It was a part of the Philippines that, for us, became inseparably linked to our summers there.

Especially the gravy that came with the chicken was something we could only get there. And the spaghetti — an unusual Filipino version with sweet tomato sauce and hotdog slices — totally won us over. Andrew and I were quite different when it came to food: I never ate fish or seafood, while Andrew couldn't get enough of it. But when it came to Jollibee, we were completely on the same page — we always looked forward to it.

Jollibee was a key part of our Philippines experience. It was technically just a fast-food restaurant, but it felt like more than that. It was a piece of the country, a place that connected us with the culture — even though it was far from traditional Filipino food.

Years later, while we were visiting Rome with our mum, we had an unexpected experience. Among all the Italian landmarks and delicious pizza, we suddenly came across — Jollibee. For us, it felt like stepping back in time to our summers in the Philippines. Of course, we had to go in right away. A little piece of the Philippines in the middle of

Rome. Andrew and I ordered fries, while our mum treated herself to the Filipino-style chicken. But as much as we tried to recreate that old feeling — it wasn't quite the same. The chicken tasted different, not like it did in the Philippines.

But that moment in Rome showed us something else: no matter where you are in the world, there are Filipinos who bring their culture — and their favorite fast-food chain — with them. Jollibee was more than just a restaurant; it was a symbol of how the Filipino diaspora carries its roots wherever it goes. For us, it was a small but special moment to realize that even in Rome, between spaghetti and pizza, a little piece of the Philippines was hiding.

VCDs

In Asia, VCDs were everywhere – a simpler, technically weaker version of DVDs. You could buy them on almost every street corner: from roadside stands to small electronics shops and even supermarkets.

When we brought our own DVDs from home for the first time, we were disappointed to find they didn't work. The region code was incorrect, and often the format didn't match the local devices. So the movies we had brought along stayed in our suitcase for the time being.

Luckily, our cousins had come prepared. They had entire stacks of VCDs – some fully legitimate, others odd "copies" with covers printed at home and films usually in English. The picture quality was often mediocre, and sometimes the movie would abruptly stop halfway through because you had to insert the second disc. But none of that spoiled the fun.

Our movie nights quickly became a regular part of family life. We sat together on the floor in front of the TV, while the adults made themselves comfortable on the couch. There was laughter, commentary, and sometimes someone would translate when something wasn't understood. It was loud, chaotic – and absolutely wonderful.

Kicker Sonderheft

Our summer trips to the Philippines often coincided with the start of the Bundesliga season. That meant the *Kicker Sonderheft* was already out in stores – an absolute must for us. *Kicker* is one of Germany's most well-known football magazines, and its special edition at the start of each season provides detailed team profiles, statistics, schedules, and expert predictions. It was a small ritual that somehow became a fixed part of our travels. The special issue was our way of looking ahead to the upcoming season, and as long-time 1. FC Nürnberg fans, we always hoped for a stable season – especially for survival in the top flight. As supporters of 1. FC Nürnberg, you had to be modest; dreams of winning the title were pretty unrealistic. But the *Kicker Sonderheft* remained a tradition that gave us just the right dose of optimism for the new season.

And with football in our luggage, we always found someone in the Philippines to talk to about the upcoming Bundesliga season. The owner of the dive shop was a passionate Karlsruhe SC fan, and the neighbors had roots in Bochum – and therefore a certain fondness for VfL Bochum. These conversations about German football brought a piece of home to the island and helped fill our summer evenings with something familiar.

The *Kicker Sonderheft* was our anchor – a small reminder that we would soon be flying off. Even today, when we see it at the start of the Bundesliga season, we both feel it: it's as if the old routine comes back to life. The magazine remains a cherished ritual – a reminder of all those summers and the journeys that lay ahead.

Chapter 9: Summer Vacation 2004

By the summer of 2004, we were fully settled into our yearly travel routine: flying from Frankfurt to Hong Kong, then on to Cebu, and finally to our island in the Philippines. As soon as we arrived, we put on the *Best of 2003* CD at home, which greeted us with songs like "Guten Tag (Die Reklamation)" by Wir Sind Helden – a track we had come to know through the FIFA video game as well. It was a familiar, relaxed time. We visited relatives, explored neighboring islands, and fully enjoyed the long summer days.

As always, our dad kept busy fixing things around the house, always finding something to improve, while our mum spent time visiting relatives and reconnecting with friends. The Fiesta, as every year, was a highlight and increasingly became a large family reunion. By then, some of our older cousins already had children of their own, who played with us every day, full of excitement and energy.

At the same time, the Olympic Games in Athens were taking place. Although the Philippines didn't win any medals that year, that would change in the years to come. So the summer of 2004 became a sporty one for us – filled with competition and fun. Between ping-pong matches, island trips, and the Fiesta, we spent carefree days in our second home.

Hike

On an especially beautiful day, we decided to go on a hike –
to a place deeply rooted in our family's history: our
grandmother's old house. The path there was anything but
easy. Starting from the beach, it took two hours uphill
through dense jungle. Our great-aunt, who knew the area
like the back of her hand, guided us along narrow
footpaths and through thick underbrush – trails that
seemed to lead us back to another time.

Along the way, we passed tiny fields, small bamboo
houses, and places completely unfamiliar to us. Here, far
from the main road, the world felt entirely different. Cars
were useless – only motorcycle taxis could manage to
transport people over the steep and bumpy terrain. For us,
it was a journey into the past, though not one entirely
frozen in time. There were still cell phones and Coca-Cola,
but it felt as if we had reached the end of the world.

When we finally arrived at the small bamboo house, we
took a break. It was a simple home – old, but lovingly
maintained and continuously repaired. Our great-aunt,
who had led us there, was already in her late sixties at the
time, but for her, this path was just part of daily life. She
had to feed the pigs that were kept there. Unlike her
siblings who had left the village, she had stayed –
surrounded by nature and the life she had always known.
These hikes were not just a duty for her, but a source of joy.
She loved caring for the old house and the animals.

After feeding the pigs, we sat down, drank fresh coconut
water, ate mangoes, and let the moment sink in. The old
house spoke of another time, of a different life we only
knew from stories. The way back was exhausting, but we

carried the memory of what we had seen and experienced like a treasure.

It was a place where time seemed to move more slowly – a place full of stories. Rarely had we felt so far from the modern world, and yet never had we felt closer to our family and its roots. It was a hike we will never forget – a moment when past and present quietly merged.

Beauty Pageants

Every year during Fiesta, beauty pageants were held in our village. However, these contests were less about serious competition and more about entertainment, with fun being the main focus. One of the most popular categories was the competition in which men dressed up as women. They struck poses, danced, and entertained the crowd with such joy that the entire village roared with laughter.

The topic of homosexuality was handled with surprising openness and ease in the Philippines – especially in contexts like this. Those who had come out lived openly and confidently, and it hardly seemed to bother anyone – a remarkable contrast to the often more reserved attitudes we knew from Germany.

Alongside these humorous competitions were also the classic beauty pageants – from Miss Southern Leyte to Miss Philippines. At the national level, the competition was intense, with contestants vying for prestigious titles like Miss Universe or Miss World. These events were followed with great enthusiasm across the country. Filipinos were especially proud in 2015 when Pia Wurtzbach, a German-Filipina, was crowned Miss Universe. The title holds great prestige in the Philippines, and Pia became a national heroine.

Beauty pageants are a firmly rooted tradition in the Philippines. Every village has its own little event, and it's not uncommon for expensive dresses to be rented and elaborate choreography to be rehearsed. Yet despite all the preparation, the focus remains on having fun. For the villagers, it's an opportunity to come together, to laugh, and to celebrate – and the joyful atmosphere is always contagious.

Poverty

Our journeys home from the Philippines back to Germany usually began with the ferry. It was a six-hour ride from Maasin, a small city on the island of Leyte, to Cebu.

We often arrived in Cebu early in the morning, and it felt like an eternity before the ferry finally docked. While we were waiting to disembark, we suddenly noticed something that would stay in our memories for years: small fishing boats appeared alongside the ferry – but they weren't occupied by fishermen. Instead, we saw mothers with small children sitting in the boats. They weren't there to fish, but to beg.

The first time we saw this, we were maybe ten or eleven years old. We watched as passengers on the ferry began tossing coins into the water, and the children in the boats immediately dove in after them, trying to catch the money before it sank. Sometimes the coins landed in the boats, but often they didn't – and then the children would dive headfirst into the sea to retrieve the change. We stood there, confused and somewhat shaken, unsure how to process what we were seeing. On one hand, it was impressive how quick and agile the children were, but on the other, it was heartbreaking to witness such desperation.

The following year, we made a plan: we decided to prepare little plastic bags with paper bills, so the kids wouldn't have to jump into the water for coins. We thought it would be safer for them – and that banknotes might be more useful than loose change. It was our small way of trying to help – or at least to make begging a little less dangerous.

But when we took the ferry to Cebu the next year, the begging boats were gone. As we later learned, the city had banned begging near the ferries for safety reasons. The children and their mothers were no longer allowed to approach the ships.

In a strange way, we were disappointed – not because we missed the sight of poverty, but because we had wanted to help the children with our little bags, and now there was no one left to give them to.

It was a lesson for us. The poverty we saw in the Philippines was everywhere. And sometimes we tried to ease it with small gestures – even though we were just children. But reality was often harsher than our childlike ideas of how to fix things could have ever imagined.

Chapter 10: Summer Vacation 2005

The summer of 2005 was overshadowed by an event from the previous year: the tsunami in the Indian Ocean in December 2004 – one of the most devastating natural disasters we had witnessed up to that point. The sheer force of the sea, which destroyed entire coastlines and villages, cast a long shadow – even in Germany, where many people were affected, including those who had traveled to Thailand over the holidays and never returned. At home, we followed the news – stunned and speechless. This event left a lasting impression on us and changed the way we viewed the sea and its power.

Although this tsunami hadn't reached the Philippines, our mother reminded us of a similar incident in the past. In 1960, she told us, a massive earthquake in Chile had sent a huge wave all the way to the Philippines – causing significant damage there. The idea that an earthquake on the other side of the world could impact our village was both fascinating and frightening.

When we arrived back in our home village in the Philippines in the summer of 2005, our first thought was how far it might be to the nearest hilltop – a place of safety. With every small earthquake – which weren't uncommon there – our eyes immediately turned to the sea, watching for signs: was the water pulling back? That could be a warning of an approaching wave. And we watched the animals around us. Animals suddenly retreating – dogs barking, monkeys heading for the hills – had become warning signs to us, a kind of built-in instinct we had developed. We had once seen a report about people who had saved their lives by observing animals. That memory stuck with us.

We also noticed something else as we looked at the village: the waves seemed to be getting higher, and during stronger storms, the water pushed dangerously close to the village. Climate change was no longer just a headline on the news – it had become a visible reality. Anyone still doubting that the world was changing only had to look at the rising high tide lines.

Despite all this, the summer of 2005 was once again a beautiful one, full of familiar moments: the Fiesta, reuniting with family, music, and relaxing on the beach. It was a time of community and peace – and despite all the worries, we looked forward to the next year with hope.

The sun is gone, but the sky still glows with a vibrant orange. In front of it: the three of us – captured in a moment that will last.

Sauerkraut

Not far from us, just a few houses down, lived another German family we knew well. Like us, they had grown up between two cultures and had also built a house for their family nearby in the Philippines. During one of their visits, they had, as is common in the Philippines, shipped several boxes of supplies ahead of time. After all, the 40-kilo baggage allowance alone wasn't enough to bring everything one might need or miss from Germany.

Shortly before their return to Germany, they casually mentioned that they still had some supplies left over that they wouldn't be able to use. "We still have twelve cans of sauerkraut," they said with a smile – as if it were the most normal thing in the world to have twelve cans of sauerkraut with you in the Philippines. At that moment, we knew exactly what that meant: a little taste of Bavaria would be served.

On the last day of our stay, just before our flight back to Germany, we decided to turn the opportunity into a celebration. A traditional German meal, right in the middle of the Philippines – that would be our farewell to this vacation. The cans of sauerkraut were opened, and we prepared everything else needed for a proper German meal: potatoes, Knöchle, smoked pork – all the things that reminded us of our Franconian roots and brought the flavors of Germany back to us one more time.

It was a wonderful meal. The sauerkraut may not have been what one would typically crave in a tropical climate – but that's exactly what made it special. It was one of those moments when we experienced a little piece of Germany in the heat of the Philippines – an unexpected contrast that made us smile. For all of us, who regularly moved between these two worlds, that sauerkraut meal on our last day became a small but meaningful reminder of how closely Germany and the Philippines were woven together in our lives.

The Carpenter

Right in the house next to ours lived the carpenter with his family – a skilled craftsman who was always there when something stuck or rattled. Whether the front door needed adjusting or the ping-pong table needed its final touches – he helped with every little task, with a calm and natural presence that simply felt like part of the neighborhood.

He didn't have the latest tools, but he had great skill – and he was always excited to use our dad's modern equipment whenever the opportunity arose.

One day, we had an idea: to take a photo of him with one of our power drills. The plan was to send the picture to a tool dealer friend in Germany – hoping it might make it into the next product catalog. A small gesture to show that these tools were truly used around the world. We already imagined showing him the catalog on our next visit to the Philippines. He would've been thrilled to see himself featured in a German tool catalog.

But like so many things, the idea fell through due to German bureaucracy. The manufacturer insisted on a written consent form in order to even consider using the photo – a detail that seemed absurd to us, since we knew him personally. But we weren't surprised. We knew how bureaucracy worked in Germany.

So in the end, the photo remained just a fond memory. And as we recently learned while writing this chapter, the carpenter has sadly since passed away.

Boy

Boy – that's what everyone called him – lived just around the corner. He was one of the men who had helped build the house – always present, always with a smile on his face.

He had a particularly close friendship with Andrew. The two of them understood each other without words. When the tide was low, they would wander together through the mudflats, collecting shells, sea urchins – sometimes just in silence. At the time, Andrew barely spoke any English, and Boy only spoke Visaya. And yet, somehow, they just clicked.

He was the kind of person who made everyone laugh. He was always telling jokes – loud, animated – and everyone would laugh along. Everyone, except maybe us. Not because it wasn't funny, but because we hardly understood a word. His language was full of life, but to us, it was often a mystery.

Of course, we always brought cigarettes for him – a popular gift. Thanks to Duty Free, they were cheaper for us, and he was always delighted, as if we had given him a small celebration. One time, we even sent him a postcard from Oktoberfest – and he was incredibly proud of it. He showed it off as if it were an official diploma.

Boy was one of those people who simply belong – without you even realizing it, until they're no longer there. He died the following year. Chronically ill, as we later found out. Too soon, too quietly – but with a smile that remains in our memory.

Detour

Anyone who travels a lot quickly learns: unexpected and unannounced extra charges sometimes just come with the territory. In the Philippines, this often happens with a smile – one that suggests you're not just paying for the service, but also for the good mood that comes with it.

One experience that especially stuck with us was a ride to the port. It should have been a straightforward trip – or so we thought. But our jeepney made an unexpected stop – not at the terminal, but at a strategically placed bicycle taxi stand. The explanation? Vehicles supposedly weren't allowed to go directly to the port. Why exactly remained unclear – especially since we later saw several jeepneys parked right at the port entrance.

The system quickly became clear: the stop ensured that the pedicab drivers also got a slice of the pie. For us, it just meant a small detour and a few extra pesos. And right on cue, the smiling drivers were already waiting, ready to load our luggage and take us the last stretch.

Of course, we went along with it – what choice did we have? So we climbed in, let ourselves be pedaled the rest of the way, and took it with good humor. No big deal, no frustration – just another one of those typical travel stories you laugh about later. And in the end, everything (and everyone) arrived just fine.

* * *

In the pedicab, with Dad and Andrew right in the middle.

And of course, I was in the pedicab too.

Chapter 11: Summer Vacation 2006

In the summer of 2006, something fundamental changed for us: we earned our diving certificates and experienced the fascinating underwater world of the Philippines for the first time. The dive center, run by a German-Filipino family, had always been a special place for us. The owner's son used every opportunity to improve his German, and each year we brought current magazines from Germany with us. After reading them, we left them at the dive center so he and the other German-speaking guests would have something to read – a small piece of Germany that stayed throughout the summer.

For us, getting our diving certificates meant gaining access to an entirely new world. For two weeks, we learned the basics of diving – from equipment and techniques to safety – and at the end, we proudly held our certification cards in our hands. It was a special feeling to see the colorful corals and fish at depths of 10 to 15 meters – an adventure that left a lasting impression on us.

We also became aware of what a privilege it is to dive in this region. Many locals who live just a few meters from the water can't afford to dive. As a result, the experience of the marine world is often reserved for wealthier Filipinos and tourists. But with the growing focus on environmental protection, efforts are being made to preserve the reefs and their biodiversity. Educational programs in schools and communities are raising awareness among locals about the importance of marine conservation. Projects on waste separation and training on how to interact with nature show that awareness is slowly shifting.

Despite all the beautiful memories, we decided to take a break in 2007 and not travel to the Philippines that summer. So the summer of 2006 remained particularly memorable in many ways – as the year of our first dive, and of an intense experience we wanted to let sink in for a while.

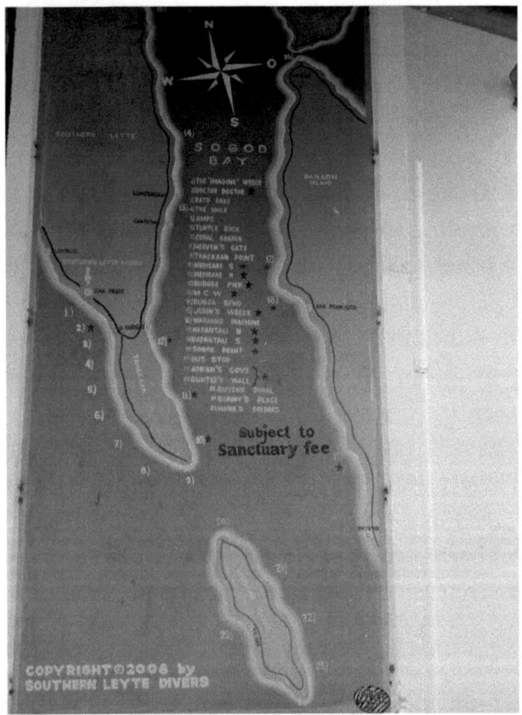

The overview map of the dive sites by "Southern Leyte Divers" – as of 2008.

Limasawa

The neighboring island of Limasawa holds an important place in history, as it was this island that Ferdinand Magellan first reached during his famous journey halfway around the world. We once took a trip there to visit the "Magellan Cross," which had been erected on a hill on the island. There wasn't much else to see on Limasawa – apart from the breathtaking beauty of its beaches and untouched nature. A small, almost forgotten gem in the ocean, it impressed with its simplicity.

But one comment from my dad stuck with me in particular: "The beer is warm," he said, surprised, when we wanted something refreshing after our hike up the hill. At that time, Limasawa had only limited electricity, generated by fuel-powered generators. So getting a cold drink wasn't something to take for granted – and for someone used to having chilled drinks anytime, it was a small surprise.

Back then, the island had electricity for only a few hours a day – just enough to power the essentials. Whether that's still the case today, I'm not entirely sure. But it would be interesting to find out if Limasawa has since switched to wind or solar energy. That would certainly suit the times, and it would make for an exciting destination on our next trip. Maybe then we'll see how the island has developed – and whether the drinks are served cold by now.

Karaoke

Just as I was casually watching *Deutschland sucht den Superstar* (a long-running German talent show where aspiring singers compete for a recording deal and national fame, similar in format to *American Idol*), a singer caught my attention. I immediately turned to my girlfriend and said, "He's Filipino!" The young man, Rendy Aprillio from Norderstedt, had barely started singing, and yet it was instantly clear. His voice, his style – it was unmistakable. Filipinos simply have this special talent for singing, and that's no coincidence.

In the Philippines, singing is more than just a hobby – it's a way of life. Karaoke machines are everywhere. Almost every household has at least one microphone, usually accompanied by a booklet of song codes and a small rating machine that scores your performance after every song. Karaoke happens everywhere: on the ferry at 3 a.m., keeping fellow passengers awake who are just trying to sleep; in the neighborhood, where the whole area is filled with music at midnight. People sing – whether in tune or not – and often with such passion that it becomes infectious.

The importance of singing in the Philippines runs deep. It's not about being perfect – it's about the feeling, the joy of the moment, the sense of togetherness. Singing brings people together, no matter where they are. It's no surprise that the current lead singer of the band *Journey*, Arnel Pineda, is Filipino – stepping into the legendary shoes of Steve Perry.

Filipinos have tremendous stage talent – and it's finally getting more recognition. Artists like Jo Koy, a Filipino-

American comedian, are making a name for themselves internationally and raising awareness of Filipino culture. It's a step in the right direction, and we hope this incredibly talented community, so close to our hearts, will become even more visible in the future.

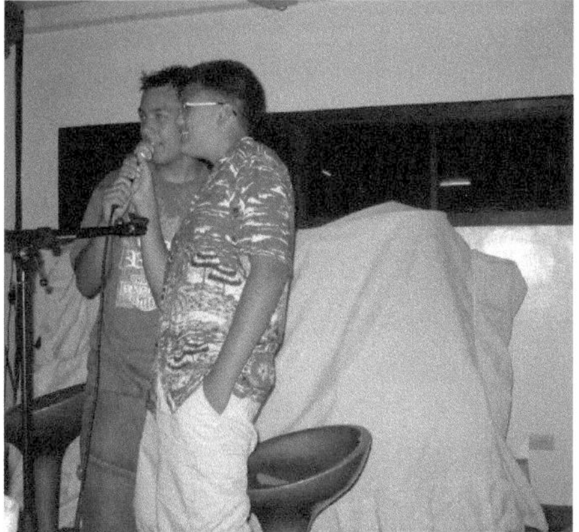

A moment from 2006: the two of us, side by side, singing our hearts out during a karaoke session – imperfect, but full of emotion.

Farewells

The farewells from the Philippines were always filled with emotion. It felt as though the country held onto us a little more tightly each time our departure approached. Our grandfather was very sad, even if he only showed his feelings quietly.

On one occasion, it felt like the entire extended family had come to the port to say goodbye: uncles, aunts, cousins – all there to send us off with warm hugs and soft-spoken farewells.

The final hours before our departure were always filled with a quiet melancholy. The suitcases were already packed, and the familiar streets and faces passed by one last time. Even our dive center became a place of parting. Again and again, the crew would ask, "Will you come back next time?" And most of the time, we answered vaguely: "We're not sure yet, but we'll try."

As long as we were still in school, the timing of our next trip was predictable – always during summer break, always the same weeks. But over the years, flight prices increased. The days of discounted child fares were over, and eventually, we had to pay the full price for four tickets. It was a considerable amount, and each year we'd cast a brief, uncertain glance back and say, "We'll have to see."

Chapter 12: Summer Vacation 2008

In 2008, we actually hadn't planned a trip to the Philippines. But then we received the news that our grandfather wasn't doing well – and we decided to drop everything and travel to be with the family. Our arrival seemed to lift his spirits: day by day, he got better, and the joy of seeing him was present in every moment we spent together.

For the first time, I had brought my laptop and showed him everything that fascinated me about it. We watched a few movies together, and I hoped to find a Wi-Fi signal somewhere so I could show him the vast world of the internet. He listened with curiosity as I explained things to him and enjoyed the time with us as if he knew these days were something special. Sometimes he would come over with drinks, and we felt that familiar sense of connection he always radiated. Mum was constantly by his side too – full of joy and relief to see her father come back to life.

We went diving, we laughed, and we made a point to be fully present during that time. As always, the dive center was a highlight – the moments underwater, the shared laughter, the stories: it all felt almost magical. We were nearly 16 and 14 years old and enjoyed the freedom of exploring the nightlife with our older cousins – halfway legal, but filled with that thrilling feeling of finally experiencing a small piece of adulthood.

This trip would also be the last time we shared the Philippines with our grandfather. Shortly after we returned to Germany, he passed away. We didn't attend the funeral – but that was okay. We had been able to say goodbye, and the last days we spent together were full of closeness and beautiful memories. The conversations, the laughter, and the small moments with him carried us through the grief and still make us think of that summer – a summer of farewell and deep connection, one that will forever remain in our hearts.

The Japanese

In our village, there was a man we simply called "the Japanese". He had come to the Philippines many years ago and built a life for himself there.

He wasn't just kind and respectful, but also a true jack-of-all-trades. There seemed to be nothing he couldn't fix. Whether it was a broken tool, a leaky pipe, or an improvised construction – he always knew how to repair it. It was as if he had a trick up his sleeve for every problem.

When he wasn't building or fixing something, we often saw him in the mornings at the beach, snorkeling with mask and fins in search of sea urchins. He always looked calm and at peace, as if he were simply drifting through the day.

He had found not only a home in the Philippines but also a family. His wife and daughter lived in the village as well.

Every year, when we returned to the Philippines, he was there – even in the later years. Now, in 2024, as I write this chapter, I spoke with our mum again and asked about him. Sadly, I found out that he has passed away.

Internet Cafés

In the early years in the Philippines, we had hardly any real connection to home. The internet, as we know it today, wasn't widely available yet, and mobile internet was practically unaffordable and rare. In the 2000s, the first internet cafés began to appear in the cities – and suddenly, we too had the chance to connect with home from time to time.

Back then, we both used SchülerVZ (a popular German social networking platform in the 2000s, designed specifically for school-aged students to connect, chat, and share updates – similar to Facebook, but tailored for younger users) and ICQ. For about two euros, we could log into one of those internet cafés for a while. It was exciting to be part of the digital world again, where birthday greetings and messages from friends awaited us – people we otherwise could rarely reach.

These cafés were especially popular – not just with us, but also with many Filipinos whose family members worked abroad. They were the most important link for all those who had loved ones in faraway countries. The days of being able to browse the digital world anytime, anywhere on a mobile device were still a long way off.

Chapter 13: Check-Out

After we had "checked out" at the airport, the next routine began right away. After every return from the Philippines, there was an unofficial unpacking get-together at our house – almost like a small celebration. It was always understood that we had brought back letters and small gifts from our distant second home, and everyone was eager to receive them. So we invited family and friends over, and often there were fresh mangoes from the Philippines that we had brought with us – along with other treats that stirred up memories.

Everyone wanted to hear about the trip, and storytelling became part of the experience itself. In the background, a video from our most recent vacation usually played – showing our cousins, outings, and celebrations. The memories seemed to come alive, and as we looked back, we almost automatically played a kind of "telephone game": news from the village that changed slightly with each retelling. "That friend from the bridge sadly passed away," or "The neighbor moved to Canada" – there was always so much to share.

Almost always, plans for the next trip started taking shape. Friends and relatives asked when we'd be flying back, and the first ideas for the following year were already being passed around. This little get-together was never just about looking back – it was also a glimpse of

what was yet to come. A moment in which, in our hearts,
one foot was already back in the Philippines.

Kirchweih

On the first Sunday of September, our hometown of Hohenfeld celebrated its annual Kirchweih – or *Kerm,* as we lovingly called it. As soon as we arrived, we were already excited to see our friends again. It marked the last carefree days before school started back up. The *Kerm* was a central part of our childhood in Franconia – the village festival where everyone gathered: friends, neighbors, and even those who had long since moved away came back for this one weekend.

The *Kerm* was more than just a celebration – it was a piece of home. When everyone came together to share stories from the summer and celebrate, that familiar sense of belonging returned year after year. It reminded us of the Fiesta in our Philippine hometown – there, too, the festival was a reason for families to reunite, share memories, and keep traditions alive.

Between pickup games on the football field and the first training sessions after the summer break, everyday life slowly returned. But the *Kerm* helped ease the transition – from the lightness of summer back into the rhythm of routine, from one world into another.

In those moments, we became aware of how deeply rooted we were in both cultures. The Franconian *Kerm* and the Filipino Fiesta – as different as they were – shared something essential: a sense of home, community, and belonging. They were two sides of the same childhood – and both returned every year like a small ritual of coming home.

Andrew and I at the Kerm in 2022 – dressed in traditional Lederhosen.

Part 2: Identities (2009 - 2013)

Grow Up

With these years, the "cassette era" finally came to an end. The familiar recordings from our childhood gave way to digital images and social media. We had arrived in the digital world – and with it, a new chapter of our lives began.

Between 2009 and 2013, we began our journey into adulthood – a time that shaped us and formed our perspectives. These were the years of our first steps toward independence: we began to travel on our own, to study, to take on our first jobs. For the first time, we earned our own money – even as we never completely lost sight of our responsibilities toward the family, despite university and work sometimes pulling us in different directions.

This stage of life was accompanied by a deeper engagement with our Filipino heritage and the social realities of our second homeland. Even though we were no longer in the Philippines during that time, we closely followed what was happening there – how the political climate was shifting and what challenges people were facing.

The older we got, the stronger our desire became to truly understand the cultural differences between Germany and the Philippines. In our early twenties, we began to see both societies through new eyes – their structures, customs, and dynamics. And with this desire to understand came the realization of how deeply Filipino culture and community were rooted in us, even though we had spent most of our lives in Germany.

This part of the book is therefore not only a chronicle of our coming of age, but also a journey into the complex –

and at times contradictory – societies to which we belong.

94

Chapter 14: Understanding Germany

Germany – an economically strong country in the heart of Europe, known for its industry, infrastructure, and role as an export nation. With around 84 million inhabitants, it is one of the most populous countries in Europe and offers many people stability, security, and educational opportunities. German society is characterized by a high degree of organization, social security, and the pursuit of individuality – yet it also faces challenges such as integration, demographic change, and growing social diversity.

This chapter offers insight into the years in which we began to understand what it means to be German – and that identity doesn't always come with a clear answer. It was a time of reflection, during which we realized that both cultures are part of who we are.

History

Germany's history is inextricably linked to the two World Wars. Even today, many families carry the memories of that time – including ours. Our grandparents lived through the Second World War: some as children in air-raid shelters, others as young people at the front or fleeing their homes. Their stories – full of fear, loss, and the will to survive – still accompany us today. They are part of our collective memory and shape the historical consciousness of many people in Germany.

At the same time, Germany is a country full of contrasts – not only culturally, but also historically and regionally. The differences between the former East and West are still noticeable decades after reunification – whether in economic prosperity, political attitudes, or people's sense of identity. In the north, the Frisians shape the coastal regions with their own language and traditions, while in Bavaria, with its Catholic-influenced culture, the Alps, traditional clothing, and customs, a very different identity is lived. In between lie cities like Berlin, Cologne, and Leipzig, where past, present, and future meet in unique ways. This field of tension is part of what defines Germany today – a country that constantly redefines itself, yet must also learn to deal with its internal differences.

In German society, remembering and understanding its own history plays a central role. National Socialism, the Holocaust, war, and destruction – all of this has profoundly shaped not only the country, but also its sense of global responsibility. Coming to terms with these dark chapters and the clear commitment to democracy, human rights, and peace have become essential parts of German identity. Education, memorials, monuments, and school curricula all help ensure that "Never again" is more than just a phrase.

But this stance is increasingly under pressure. An openly far-right party is gaining more and more support – in some regions, it has already become the strongest political force. Racism, antisemitism, and nationalist rhetoric – once thought to be overcome – are re-emerging in everyday life and even entering parliaments. In the Bundestag of 2025, only 11.6% of members of parliament have a migration background, even though nearly 30% of the population have migration experiences themselves or through their parents.

This imbalance becomes even more evident at the local level: in many city and municipal councils, people with migrant backgrounds are barely represented. It often feels as if there is an invisible wall between politics and society – between those who make decisions and those who are left to watch. This lack of representation worries us. Because those who don't have a seat at the table often have their perspectives overlooked. A diverse society also needs a diverse political voice – everywhere, not just on paper.

To understand history also means to learn from it and to remain vigilant. But this awareness seems to be fading in parts of society. That makes it all the more important to actively work toward a diverse, just, and democratic future – so that the mistakes of the past are not repeated.

Club

In our hometown of Hohenfeld, we always felt a true sense of belonging. This was where we grew up – where our friends, our family, and the community that shaped us lived. It was our first home – a place where we not only spoke the language fluently, but had also internalized the traditions and the spirit of togetherness.

Being part of this community naturally meant getting involved in local clubs. From an early age, we played football and table tennis in the local sports club, moving through nearly all the youth teams before eventually joining the adult leagues. It was simply part of life for us to help out at club events and – as is expected of "real Germans" – to volunteer our time. The *Kirchweih* or the midsummer bonfire were yearly highlights. Even today, we still help out whenever our time allows.

Club life is the heart of a village community. It creates lifelong bonds and gives you a deep sense of belonging. For anyone arriving in Germany and looking to integrate, there's hardly anything more valuable than becoming part of a club. A small piece of advice to all who are building a new home here: get involved in a club! Send your children to play football, handball, or join another sports team. Club life means solidarity – and it's the path to putting down real roots.

Our parents, especially our father, supported us from the very beginning. He was our biggest fan, our driver, and often our motivator. Especially when we started working as referees, we relied on those drives – and our father was always there, even long after we were able to drive ourselves.

Today, we often run into people we knew back then –
old teammates, acquaintances from the village, and former
referees who remind us of the moments we shared. These
are fond memories of a real sense of community, passed
down from generation to generation. Anyone who wants
to truly arrive in Germany should experience club life – it's
where real roots are planted and a true home is created.

Referees

At the age of 14, we decided to become football referees. Our local club was in urgent need of support, and since we had always felt deeply connected to it, taking on this role felt natural to us. The years we spent as referees taught us a lot – about responsibility, decisiveness, and perseverance.

Being a referee, especially at a young age, is a real challenge. At 14, we often officiated matches for players our own age or even older. At first, we were nervous – the responsibility was immense, and every game brought tension. As a referee, you have to make split-second decisions, read the game, and understand the players. Mistakes are part of it – just like in the Bundesliga, despite all the modern technology.

Through refereeing, you quickly became known in the local football scene – and that also came with unpleasant experiences. Sadly, racism in football, even in Germany, is still an issue. We often heard racist jokes and comments circulating in clubs or on Facebook groups. We tried to brush it off – but inside, it hurt. Words like that sting, especially when they come from people you respected or considered friends.

We don't want to repeat those remarks in this book. But one message is important to us: ignoring racism or staying silent – especially in clubs or football environments – allows this behavior to persist. We all need to have the courage to speak up in those moments. A simple word, a brief comment, can be a big help to those affected – and it sends a clear message that discrimination has no place in our community.

Those years as referees shaped us. They weren't always easy, but they made us stronger – and they showed us how important it is to stand tall and speak up for yourself and for others, both on and off the pitch. Today, we are no longer referees.

Foreigners

Some things just stick with you – like the way people talk about "the foreigners" or "the Muslims," both in private conversations and in public discourse. It's no surprise that far-right parties are gaining more and more support in Germany. Many people prefer to live in familiar surroundings. But we also live in a democracy, where everyone can – and should – participate. This is precisely where populists find their stage, often with absurdly simplistic claims about "the foreigners," who are collectively blamed for all sorts of problems. Sometimes it's hard for us to understand how such ideas can reach – and convince – so many people.

We both went to school in Germany, in classrooms shaped by a diversity of nationalities and cultures. That mix was an enrichment for all of us. It was always exciting when friends shared stories about their roots – whether it was someone's Turkish heritage or another's Pakistani family background. But after school, many people seem to lose contact with other cultures, and the openness that once existed often gives way to a retreat into the familiar. That's when "normal life" begins – apprenticeships, jobs, everyday routines – and with it, the constant pursuit of security and stability. And that's exactly where prejudice finds its way in: through oversimplified news, subtle mistrust, and often just a lack of understanding of anything unfamiliar.

We ourselves have experienced such prejudices and hostilities – not only online, but also in real life. In those moments, it becomes clear how deeply rooted these attitudes are, even when they're expressed only in whispers or behind closed doors.

The German constitution and the democratic values that define the country clearly speak against such thinking. But when parties and organizations disregard those values, their influence quickly rubs off on others – and what should be a Germany for everyone begins to turn into a Germany only for so-called "real Germans."

German Language

For many Filipinos who come to Germany, the German language is a real challenge. You could call it a major obstacle – because German, as anyone who has ever dealt with it knows, is a difficult language. With all its rules, cases, articles, and countless exceptions, it often feels like navigating a massive obstacle course. But one thing you'll rarely see is a Filipino living here who isn't trying to learn German. And not just that – they're always striving to improve. That's admirable and deserves respect.

We've seen this not only among Filipinos, but also among many others who weren't born in Germany. They often speak with a charming dialect or accent that reveals their roots. It's clear that German isn't their native language – but the effort they put into communicating in it is truly impressive.

However, when we look back on our childhood, that effort wasn't always met with ease or understanding. Sometimes, it felt like people who didn't speak perfect German didn't receive the patience or support they deserved. Yet German is, above all, a tool – a tool for arriving, for communicating, for connecting. And it doesn't need to be "Goethe-level German" or the polished language of a senior civil servant with a perfectly trimmed front yard. Simple German is more than enough – what really matters is that we understand each other.

This brings us to an important appeal: help those who are still learning. Support them instead of treating them condescendingly. Sadly, we've often seen people respond with impatience or mockery when someone doesn't speak German flawlessly. And here lies a strange irony: it's often those who mock others who can't speak a second language themselves – while the person they're laughing at speaks at least two, if not more. That alone should make us think.

Language is a tool for connection, not exclusion. The German language doesn't have to be a heavy burden – it just needs to be understandable. And if we make the effort to understand one another, we'll be able to learn so much more from each other.

Education

Gaps in education and a lack of understanding of different ways of life are things we've encountered time and again in Germany – and often, you only become truly aware of them in specific situations. One such moment came after the Indian Ocean tsunami in 2004. We were frequently asked if everything was okay with us. Again and again, we had to explain that the Philippines are in the Pacific, not the Indian Ocean.

Of course, the concern was well-intentioned, and it's perfectly okay not to know every geographical detail. Those questions showed genuine compassion – and we appreciated that. Still, it made us realize how important better geography education would be. One should know the world before trying to understand it.

Another memory was less harmless – it left us speechless. After the devastating Typhoon Haiyan in 2013, we overheard a comment that deeply shook us: "Why do people even live there? Why don't they just move to a safer area?" Followed by: "It's their own fault if they live there." These remarks didn't just reveal ignorance – they reflected a disturbing lack of empathy. There was no understanding of life beyond one's own comfort zone – no awareness of how the world functions outside the safety of a well-kept backyard.

We came to realize that many people in Germany live in a kind of "bubble." They tend to stay within closed social circles, surround themselves with people like themselves, and if they travel at all, it's usually through package holidays or cruises. In these sheltered vacation worlds, they continue speaking German, stick to what they know, and avoid truly seeing the world outside.

But this leads to a distorted view of reality. For many, it's unimaginable that there are places in the world where people simply can't relocate – because there are no alternatives, or because poverty makes any option impossible.

People in the Philippines have always lived with nature – with storms, monsoons, and earthquakes. These dangers are part of daily life. And while they must cope with them, they also bear the brunt of the climate crisis – a crisis they've contributed little to. While industrialized nations like Germany escape the worst effects and continue running coal power plants or driving large cars, countries like the Philippines face floods, typhoons, and rising sea levels – with consequences that cost lives and livelihoods.

There is an urgent need for more awareness and less ignorance. More understanding that not everyone in this world has the freedom to just "move somewhere safer." The world is more complex – and often harsher – than it appears from the comfort of a living room.

Mismatched Couple

"Old German dad, young Filipina mum" – a common cliché that we've encountered personally. Our mum is 18 years younger than our dad. There was plenty of whispering behind closed doors, and of course, we noticed it: "What does a young woman want with an old man?" or similar remarks. We're not deaf. But beyond all the gossip and prejudice, the real story behind it is often much deeper – and it's one that many of our German-Filipino friends share.

In the 1980s and 1990s, there were indeed intermediaries who connected single German men with Filipina women. Today, it's more commonly done online. Back then, it happened through letters, long phone calls, and a lot of courage on both sides. If things felt right, the woman would eventually be invited to Germany – and often, this new life began at Frankfurt Airport. He was looking for a partner; she was too – and, of course, also for a better life. It was a mix of hope and pragmatism, and for many, it marked the beginning of a new chapter.

These relationships may not have started with the kind of romance we see in the movies. But when we think of the many German-Filipino families we know, we think of warmth, connection, and love. These couples built lives together, started families, and created something lasting. The celebrations we shared in large gatherings were full of joy, sincerity, and strong bonds. Sometimes, love doesn't start with fireworks – it grows over the years: through shared decisions, through the challenges faced together, and through everyday life.

One thought keeps coming up when we think about the

clichés: the divorce rate in Germany in 2023 was 35.75%. And it certainly isn't being driven up by German-Filipino families. It's easy to judge from the outside: "Where else would she go? They have no money, blah blah blah." But one thing should never be forgotten: you can recognize a happy family. You can recognize true love. Always.

Many of the fathers of our German-Filipino friends have already passed away, and with each loss, a space is left behind that everyone feels. It's not just an empty chair – it's missing stories, laughter, and the quiet, steady love that held these families together.

And in those moments, we understand that these relationships were far more than clichés and stereotypes. They were real bonds, lasting for decades, creating families – and growing into a kind of love that even carries the pain of loss within it.

Chapter 15: Understanding Philippines

The Philippines – an archipelago of over 7,000 islands with around 115 million inhabitants and a rich, multicultural history. To truly understand this country, one must look beyond the beautiful beaches and vibrant markets. It's about getting to know a society deeply shaped by religious faith, colonial influences, and a strong sense of community – especially rooted in family and neighborhood life.

In this chapter, we take a closer look at the everyday lives of people in the Philippines. What drives them? Why do so many work abroad? Millions of Filipinos earn their living far from home as so-called Overseas Filipino Workers. They are not only a major economic force, but also a reflection of deep family responsibility – often accompanied by significant personal sacrifice.

Our goal is to present the Philippines in all its complexity – from political and economic developments to the everyday stories, traditions, and values of its people. To understand the Philippines means discovering a country balancing tradition and modernity – where family, solidarity, and cultural identity remain at the heart of life.

History

The history of the Philippines, much like that of Germany, has been shaped by war and colonial rule – two countries geographically far apart, yet uniquely connected through the events of the 20th century. Our Filipino grandparents, just like our German ones, lived through the Second World War. While Europe suffered under the consequences of National Socialism and the war, the Philippines endured Japanese occupation – a period deeply etched into the collective memory. The war spared no continent: destruction, fear, and suffering were a harsh reality on the islands as well. That both countries were caught up in the conflict highlights just how truly global this war was.

But the history of the Philippines extends far beyond this dark chapter. More than a thousand years ago, the islands were already a vibrant hub for seafarers, traders, and cultures from around the world. Arab, Chinese, Indian, and later Malay ships brought not only goods, but also ideas, languages, and influences that continue to resonate today. Long before European colonization, the archipelago was part of a vast maritime network.

Starting in the 16th century, Spain ruled the country for over 300 years – a colonial legacy still visible in many aspects of life. The Catholic Church continues to play a central role in both public and private spheres, with festivals, customs, and rituals strongly shaped by Spanish traditions. Linguistically, Spanish influence is especially noticeable in the Visayas region.

After Spanish rule ended, the United States took control of the Philippines. The introduction of the American education system, the spread of the English language, and a

Western-influenced lifestyle created a new social reality –
many of these influences remain part of everyday life
today.

This complex past has shaped Filipino identity into a
layered tapestry – marked by ancient cultures, colonial
domination, and the struggle for independence. As in
Germany, the experiences of war and foreign rule continue
to echo into the present in the Philippines. The stories of
our grandparents – whether from Europe or Asia – remind
us how deeply history shapes our lives today, and how
important it is to know it and pass it on.

Climate Change

Typhoon Haiyan – known in the Philippines as Yolanda – is deeply etched into our memory. It was November 2013 when one of the strongest tropical cyclones ever recorded made landfall. More than 10,000 people lost their lives in the disaster – a number almost impossible to comprehend. Haiyan was set to strike the very region where our family and many friends live. Our small village, San Roque, suddenly lay directly in the storm's predicted path. The days leading up to it were filled with worry and uncertainty. All we could do from afar was watch helplessly and hope.

At the time, I was in Zurich for a six-month internship. That weekend, I was on my way back to Germany when I began following the first reports about the typhoon. I kept trying to get updates and reach my family – but nothing got through. For days, there was complete radio silence. The uncertainty was unbearable. When the first message finally came through, we were beyond relieved: our family was safe. But the scars left by the storm were everywhere – not just in the destroyed homes, but deep within the people.

As Haiyan barreled toward the Philippines at full force, it seemed for a long time that our village would be directly hit. But at the last moment, the storm shifted direction and struck the city of Tacloban with full force. It was almost completely destroyed. It could have been us – our home, our family. But instead, it hit others. The devastation was indescribable.

The images after the storm were shocking. In Tacloban, houses lay in ruins, many people were left homeless, entire neighborhoods wiped out. Nature had changed the lives of thousands within just a few hours. Our village wasn't spared either. Many homes were damaged, the power was out for weeks, and daily life came to a complete standstill.

In the years that followed, we heard about the relief efforts of *Kinderhilfe Philippinen*, which helped rebuild schools in northern Leyte. They gave children who had lost everything in the typhoon new hope and a future. The organization is a powerful example of how effective international aid can be when used wisely. (More on this in Chapter 24.)

Haiyan was not just a terrible storm – it also stands as a symbol of how tangible the effects of climate change already are. The Philippines is one of the countries most severely affected by extreme weather. Each new typhoon highlights how vulnerable island nations are – and how urgent it is to take collective global action against climate change. And yet, despite all the destruction, the people of the Philippines continue to show courage, solidarity, and the will to rebuild – even after the worst of disasters.

A sight that is sadly becoming more and more common. Climate change is hitting the Philippines especially hard.

Facebook

By the late 2000s, we noticed that it felt like everyone in the Philippines was on Facebook. It was a real game changer that completely transformed how we stayed connected with our family. Suddenly, we could connect with all our relatives – even if we hadn't been to the Philippines in years. Through Facebook, we saw family photos, watched cousins grow up, and recognized kids we once knew from kindergarten suddenly appearing on our feeds. For the Filipino community, Facebook quickly became a kind of digital home.

But alongside the joy of this new connection came the other side of the coin. Facebook use in the Philippines is excessive – nearly every post, event, or thought is shared, liked, and commented on. For many mobile plans, only Facebook is free to use. In the early days, this was convenient – but this exclusive access has consequences: for many, the platform becomes their only source of information. Fake news and political propaganda thrive in this environment, targeting a population that is often especially vulnerable to such content. This became particularly evident during recent presidential elections, where Facebook played a decisive role.

This problem is further intensified by the political system in the Philippines. Corruption remains widespread; it's no secret that votes are sometimes bought, and that political power often serves interests far removed from those of the people. Many voters are swayed by small gifts or cash payments – a practice that everyone is aware of and that rarely happens behind closed doors.

Despite all these issues, Facebook remains the central

platform – for many, it is synonymous with "the Internet." The news feed is a window to the world – and to family. Mixed in with family photos from Canada and Australia, videos from the last fiesta, and birthday greetings are political posts shared by one side or the other. For many, Facebook is not just a social network – it's their main source of information.

Looking back, one conclusion stands out: this dependency is a real problem. The connection to family and the sharing of memories is valuable – but when Facebook becomes the only window to the world, critical thinking fades. And with that, manipulation gains power.

Education

It was one of those strange moments that stays with you for a long time. We were out with our dad when a distant acquaintance approached us and greeted us with a phrase that, for good reason, is banned in Germany. There was no ill intent – that was immediately clear to us. But while our father politely steered the conversation in another direction, we children were left speechless and confused. The words referenced something that is a clear taboo in Germany, yet in the Philippines, it was obvious that the meaning wasn't fully understood. There was a certain fascination with Germany – but one often shaped by misunderstandings and a lack of knowledge.

That episode made us reflect on the gaps in education that still exist in the Philippines. Later, when someone asked us when we were flying back to "West Germany," we realized just how outdated and distorted the understanding of Germany can sometimes be.

While education in the Philippines is technically free, and many children do have the chance to receive a solid education, there are also many who leave school early to work and support their families – especially in rural areas, where this is still a common reality. This early interruption in schooling often leads to a lack of basic knowledge about history and global affairs.

In today's world, where social media plays a central role, this issue is further amplified. Misinformation and oversimplified narratives spread quickly – and without a strong educational foundation, it becomes difficult to distinguish fact from distortion.

On the other hand, the Philippines is also home to many

private and international schools that offer excellent education. But these schools are expensive and typically accessible only to a small, privileged portion of the population – widening the gap between those who are well-informed and those who must rely on half-truths.

Politics

Politics in the Philippines is something we've encountered time and again, and we've often questioned the peculiarities of its political system. The country follows a presidential model, but perhaps the most accurate description is this: a small, powerful elite often holds the reins. Still, civil society has shown that it is not powerless. A historic example is the ousting of Ferdinand Marcos, who ruled the country for years, practically as a dictator. When Marcos was forced into exile in 1986, he left behind a trail of abuse of power and corruption – and quite literally thousands of shoes belonging to his wife, Imelda. For many Filipinos, that moment became a symbol of liberation from years of oppression marked by the absence of press freedom and the persecution of dissenters.

After Marcos, the country entered a period of transition, led by various presidents. But democracy in the Philippines remains fragile and vulnerable. After years of progress, Rodrigo Duterte rose to power – a radical figure whose "iron fist" approach and controversial methods deeply polarized the nation. Duterte's influence, along with his skillful use of social media, ultimately helped pave the way for the Marcos family's return to power.

As of 2025, Ferdinand "Bongbong" Marcos Jr. is president – the son of the former dictator. His return to the top office reflects a dangerous trend: the past is being rewritten. Increasingly, teachers and students report that the era of dictatorship is being downplayed or omitted entirely from history books. Many young people today are hearing a new version of the story – one in which the crimes, suffering, and voices of the victims are largely absent. It is a quiet attempt to erase a critical chapter of Philippine history from collective memory.

We understand that this topic divides many Filipinos. It's not a comfortable subject – but it is a necessary one. Because democracy is the best alternative we have – and it must be protected. The myth of the "strongman" may be tempting to many, but it often thrives on false promises and grand illusions.

Journalism

Journalism in the Philippines is a daily balancing act between truth and danger. The work of many journalists in the country is repeatedly hindered by powerful interests, and the challenges they face are immense. One outstanding example of investigative journalism is the online platform Rappler – a media outlet that, despite constant resistance, remains firmly committed to the truth. In 2021, Maria Ressa and Rappler were awarded the Nobel Peace Prize for their courageous efforts. But this award was not only a recognition of the outlet itself – it also became a symbol for the many journalists in the Philippines who work under extremely dangerous conditions to expose corruption and abuse of power.

According to Reporters Without Borders, there are around 600 radio stations and 500 newspapers in the Philippines – a number that suggests a remarkable diversity of media. However, most of these private outlets are owned by influential families and business tycoons who primarily serve their own interests. While tabloid journalism often garners attention with sensational headlines, critical journalists must fear severe consequences for their work.

Press freedom in the Philippines is under serious threat, as reflected in international rankings: in the 2024 World Press Freedom Index, the Philippines ranked 134th out of 180 countries – a sobering position that reveals just how difficult and dangerous the fight for truth really is. The apparent media diversity often masks the reality that press freedom in the Philippines is fragile at best. In a landscape dominated by power interests and deliberate disinformation, journalists fight every day for independent reporting. Their work is not only essential to democracy but also a vital source of truth for Philippine society – and it demonstrates just how brave and determined the fight for freedom can be.

Church

The Roman Catholic Church holds a significant place in Philippine society. The country is one of the largest Christian nations in the world – something that has not gone unnoticed in Rome. When we visited Rome ourselves, we often encountered Filipino clergy who greeted us warmly. The deeply rooted faith of the Filipino people was on full display in 2015, when the Pope celebrated Mass in Manila before more than six million people. For many, the Church is a steady anchor – a source of hope and comfort, especially in times marked by poverty and other challenges.

Yet there are contradictions. In an increasingly enlightened and modern world, questions arise about how conservative rules – such as priestly celibacy – fit into contemporary life. We once witnessed a priest who had to leave his ministry after falling in love. It was a painful farewell for him, as he had lived his vocation with deep passion. But the Roman Catholic Church allowed no exceptions, and the community lost a beloved spiritual leader who had inspired many.

This tension is increasingly being addressed by independent churches and religious sects that break away from the strict style of the Catholic Church, appealing to many with more open approaches. In recent years, more and more such communities have emerged, offering an alternative for those who feel disconnected from traditional religious rules.

Another important aspect of the Philippines' religious landscape is its diversity. Alongside Catholicism, ancient indigenous belief systems still exist, and the southern region of the country is home to a large Muslim minority. Ethnic and religious tensions have, at times, led to conflict and unrest in recent decades. Memories of kidnappings and attacks – such as the abduction of a German family in 2000 – have stayed with us as well.

Despite these complexities, the Church remains an important source of stability for many – a constant presence that strengthens unity in both good and difficult times, and that gives Philippine culture much of its depth and resilience.

Overseas Filipino Workers

Over two million Filipinos officially live and work abroad as so-called Overseas Filipino Workers (OFWs). However, if we include the many families who have permanently migrated and built new lives in Europe, Australia, the United States, or Canada, the global Filipino diaspora exceeds ten million people. Many of these families continue to support their relatives in the Philippines – financially, emotionally, and by maintaining close family ties across continents.

The stories of Filipinos living abroad are marked by pride and hope – but also significant sacrifice. OFWs work in a wide range of industries: as caregivers, on cruise ships, in hotels, restaurants, or private households. Their work, and especially the remittances they send back, form a vital pillar of the Philippine economy. For countless families, this income is essential – it secures daily life, enables education, and gives many children a chance at a better future.

One key reason for the international demand for Filipino workers is their strong command of English. English is an official language in the Philippines, which greatly facilitates access to global job markets. But the cost of this path is high.

For many, living and working abroad means years of painful separation from their families. Children grow up without a mother or father, relationships are maintained at a distance, and "home" is reduced to photos, video calls, and memories. Holidays, birthdays, and milestones like a child's first day of school are experienced from afar – and even the strongest internet connection cannot replace the feeling of being close.

These long separations leave deep marks. Relationships suffer, misunderstandings arise, and trust is tested. All too often, marriages and families break under the strain. Some OFWs return home after years and realize that the connection with their family is no longer what it once was – estranged by the long period of physical absence.

Despite all these challenges, the desire to offer one's family a better future remains central for many. The hope that the sacrifice is worth it carries them through the years. The pride of taking responsibility, and the rare but precious reunions with loved ones, provide both comfort and motivation. But the life away from home is – and remains – a heavy burden, one that millions of Filipinos carry with them every single day.

Noberto

It's an image that has stayed with us ever since: a segment on the German TV program *Weltspiegel* (a journalistic foreign-reporting show by ARD that highlights international events and everyday realities around the world) featured a story about Noberto, a man living in the slums of Manila. We watched as he collected leftover food from large restaurant chains to cook meals for his family. Every day, Noberto would scour piles of garbage, searching for scraps that he turned into simple dishes and then sold – a symbol of survival in the face of extreme poverty. His daily life was a struggle that deeply moved us.

Unfortunately, the segment can no longer be found online – not even in the ARD media library. An archive to preserve such reports would be invaluable, ensuring that stories like Noberto's are not forgotten. Documentaries like this shine a light on a side of the world that rarely takes center stage – a reality that is harsh and unjust, affecting millions of people.

Noberto's story powerfully showed us just how difficult life in the Philippines can be – especially for the many people who fight every day just to survive. Without money, you are often worth nothing – a harsh truth in the Philippines, as in many parts of the world.

And yet, despite these conditions, Noberto holds on to his humanity. A small smile, a kind word – even amid the most difficult circumstances, people like him preserve a sense of dignity that inspires us and reminds us how essential compassion and respect are, no matter where we are in the world.

Cash

When we landed in the Philippines, everything seemed normal at first. But shortly after our arrival, we noticed that two of our suitcases were missing. So, we went straight to the airport counter to ask about them. The response was brief: "We don't know where the bags are." It felt like there was little interest in actually solving the problem.

Then my mum gave me a subtle signal, and I immediately knew what she meant. A little cash makes things move faster. We discreetly handed the staff member 10 euros. Suddenly, the tone changed, and we were promised, "The bags will arrive tomorrow." And indeed – the next day, they were delivered to us.

This story reflects many of the experiences that shaped us in the Philippines. Another example: a school was built, but instead of using the planned amount of steel beams, less material was used. The consequences became clear during a later typhoon – the building couldn't withstand the forces. Or take road construction projects, where the concrete layer was about 30% thinner than originally agreed upon. Of course, such roads don't last long, but no one seems to care – at least not those who benefit from it.

Or consider ferry tickets during the Christmas season. Although the terminals officially sell tickets, they are mysteriously "sold out" a week before Christmas. The only way to get a ticket is through an "unofficial vendor" – at a significantly higher price, of course.

This phenomenon is by no means unique to the Philippines. A friend from Southeast Europe once told us a similar story: a police officer wanted to "double-check" his passport. A subtle glance at the passport with a 50-euro bill inside, and suddenly the inspection was over in seconds.

Thankfully, such cases have become less frequent – but they still leave a mark. In a country where the gap between rich and poor is enormous, many things don't work through clear rules and trust, but through cash. Time and again, there are situations where money serves as a "fast-track solution" to get things done.

Chapter 16: Expat-Guide

The question of whether we would ever emigrate was never really a serious consideration for either of us. Germany is and will always be our home. But the topic of emigration is fascinating – especially when you see the many reality TV shows about it. For anyone seriously considering a life in the Philippines, there are some important points to keep in mind. So here's a little guide:

1. Filipino Contacts

One thing is clear: without close family ties or truly strong friendships, it's difficult to settle permanently in the Philippines. A good example is buying property – it's strictly regulated and generally only permitted for Filipino citizens. Without family support or a trusted local contact, especially when it comes to building networks, things can quickly become complicated.

2. Trust, but not blindly.

It might sound like something from a reality TV show: a German expat is left by his Filipina partner and suddenly finds himself with five children and empty bank accounts. Stories like these are not uncommon. In the Philippines, you need trust – but also a healthy dose of caution. A small example: when someone says, "I'll finish the wall tomorrow, but I need an advance," it often means, "I need the money today, but the wall might not be done until the day after tomorrow." That might sound off-putting, but life in the Philippines follows a different rhythm. Time isn't measured as strictly as it is in Germany. In fact, many expats feel at ease for precisely that reason – they're escaping the pressure of time clocks and rigid punctuality.

3. Learning the Language

Even though you can get by quite well with English in the Philippines, you only truly arrive when you speak the local language. Learning some Tagalog or Visayan opens doors and shows that you take the country and its people seriously. It offers a much deeper cultural understanding and helps with integration.

4. A Purpose in Life

One point that is often underestimated is personal motivation. Many expats move to a "paradise under palm trees" and end up becoming alcoholics. Why? Because they have no purpose. No matter how beautiful the weather or how relaxed life may seem, people need a sense of direction and meaning. Opening a small guesthouse, running a dive school – these are popular ideas. But even those require full commitment, capital, and a lot of patience. Life in the Philippines works differently, and anyone who moves there must be ready to respect those cultural differences.

5. Money

Anyone planning to emigrate to the Philippines shouldn't arrive with just €1,000 in their bank account. The reality is:

you need a solid financial cushion. A mid five-figure sum is no exaggeration if you want to start off well and have reserves for emergencies. Hospitals and doctors offering quality medical care cost money. And the cost of living has risen significantly in recent years. For expats, one rule holds true: without money, nothing works here.

If you take all of this into account, there's a good chance that life in the Philippines will work out – and that the "paradise" will remain one in the long run.

P**ART** 3: F**AMILY** (2014 - 2024)

San Diego

In 2014, I spent four weeks in San Diego visiting the German side of my family, who had emigrated to the United States a few years earlier. San Diego is a beautiful city on the Pacific, right on the border with Mexico. I was fortunate to stay with my aunt and her family. After many years, I was also reunited with other relatives, and we shared a wonderful time together.

Since I had missed the beach – it had been a long time since my last trip to the Philippines – I found myself drawn to the ocean almost every day. It was only about a 15-minute walk away. Even there, I felt connected to my roots: San Diego is home to a large Filipino community. Many of its members are of mixed heritage; some have fathers or grandfathers who once served in the U.S. military and later settled in the United States. This development is closely tied to history: in the early 20th century, the Philippines was colonized by the United States – a legacy that still echoes today, not least through the continued presence of the U.S. military on the islands.

A special highlight was visiting a large Filipino supermarket – a place filled with familiar smells, familiar products, and memories. Among all the groceries, we also found Filipino beer and the iconic rum that has since gained international recognition. I toasted with my uncle that day – a moment that has stayed vividly in my memory ever since. Even though I no longer drink alcohol, I still think back on it fondly.

On my last day in San Diego, I stood at Imperial Beach as a red glow stretched across the sky – just after the sun had sunk into the sea. Alone at the shoreline, I let my gaze wander across the vast ocean. In my mind, I traveled far out over the Pacific, back toward the Philippines. After seven long years, I was finally going to return.

Chapter 17: August 2015

In 2015, we finally returned to the Philippines after seven long years. The longing had built up over all that time, and this time, we wanted to truly enjoy the journey. That's why we planned a stopover in Singapore on the way back. Part of our family lived there, and the thought of seeing them again – and exploring this fascinating city – made the trip even more exciting.

Back in the Philippines, much felt familiar – and yet, some things had changed. The people we remembered so vividly had grown older. Especially our cousin's children – once tiny babies we had held in our arms – now stood before us as almost teenagers. Of course, we had "seen" each other over the years on Facebook, but experiencing them in person was something entirely different.

We arrived in August, which meant that, as tradition dictates, I went to church at six in the morning on my birthday. Everywhere, it was "Happy Fiesta" once again, and I had the joy of experiencing the old customs that had stayed so familiar to me over the years. It was a special feeling to walk through the streets and occasionally be recognized – almost as if we had never been away. We had, of course, changed – apart from the seven extra years we brought with us – but our connection to this place felt more alive than ever.

The dive center in San Roque was once again an

essential part of our stay. We hadn't been diving since our last visit, and it felt almost nostalgic to slip back into the water. The variety of dive spots was impressive – and yet each dive was a new adventure, as the sea revealed a different side of itself every time.

This trip felt like a dream. Now, as I write these lines, I miss the sea and the time we shared there more than words can express. It was a summer full of reunions, laughter, and new memories – ones that will echo within us for a long time to come.

For the first time in seven years, back at the beach of San Roque – 2015

Schafkopf

Our dad taught us how to play *Schafkopf* – the traditional Bavarian card game that, for many, is more than just a pastime. It's a piece of culture, a ritual, and for us, it became a daily tradition in the Philippines. Almost every evening, the three of us would sit together while the wind rustled through the palm trees and the chirping of crickets filled the quiet night.

Schafkopf is usually played with four people, but since our mum had little interest in the game and our Filipino friends found it too complicated, we adjusted the rules. With a bit of creativity and our dad's guidance, the game worked surprisingly well with three players.

The funny thing is: we hardly ever played it in Germany. Maybe because, for us, it was tied to the Philippines – to those shared moments in our second home. There, far from everyday life, the card game became a regular part of our family time.

After a long break – seven years, to be exact – we sat down again in 2015 to play Schafkopf. It felt almost magical how quickly the old moves, terms, and the joy of the game came rushing back. "Ich spiele einen Wenz" or "Vier Laufende" echoed across the veranda, and time seemed to stand still.

We could see how happy our dad was that we had revived this tradition. In the years before, we had been home less often – studies and work had kept us busy. But here, on the veranda, in the tropical warmth, we found our way back to one another.

Our Schafkopf games became more than just a game. They became a symbol of our bond as a family – of the moments that brought us back together, despite the miles and the years that sometimes separated us. It felt as if we had never stopped playing. Schafkopf remained a piece of home that we carry in our hearts.

Andrew and Dad enjoying sea urchin – in the front right, right next to the San Miguel beer, you can see the Bavarian playing cards. Of course, right after this photo was taken, the card game continued.

The Coconut Bet

When Jürgen came to visit – a close family friend and the head of *Kinderhilfe Philippinen* (more on that in Chapter 24) – one thing was certain: our mum would bake her famous Gugelhupf. A true classic of German baking, and one that Jürgen especially appreciated. With coffee and cake in front of him, he would take a seat and share the story of the coconut bet.

It was one of those stories that kept resurfacing and never quite let us go: the coconut bet on the German TV show *Wetten, dass..?*, filmed in Mallorca in 2011. At the time, all we knew was that the contestant – who managed to crack five coconuts with his teeth in under two minutes – came from the Philippines. He didn't win the title of *Wettkönig* (Bet King), but he amazed the audience with his incredible performance. We wouldn't learn the full story behind it until four years later – and suddenly, it became even more fascinating.

As it turned out, the contestant came from a neighboring island. Jürgen later told us how he had accompanied him to Mallorca, and about all the challenges they had faced along the way. The journey was anything but easy: it began with tedious visa applications, endless paperwork, and long waiting times – and ended with an exhausting trip to Europe. It was a grueling process, but in the end, a great adventure. Some details remained unclear – we never heard the full version – but one thing was obvious: it had been a once-in-a-lifetime experience for him.

His appearance on *Wetten, dass..?* was a true highlight. You can still find the segment on YouTube, in the episode from June 18, 2011, where he cracked coconuts with his teeth and left the audience in awe. Even though he didn't take home the *Bet King* title, he was well rewarded. We don't remember the exact amount he received, but it was enough to provide him with a comfortable life back in the Philippines.

Later, we tried to find out whether he had appeared in any other shows or competitions, but the trail went cold. If anyone has more information, it would be fascinating to know what became of him.

Chapter 18: Stopovers

On our way back from the Philippines, we made a planned stopover in Singapore. It was a wonderful way to end our trip, and reconnecting with family made the stay especially meaningful. We met many relatives, and with our mum's cousin, we immediately began making new plans: the following year, he and his wife would visit us in Germany – and of course, a trip to Neuschwanstein Castle would be part of it. And that's exactly what happened.

We, too, made plans for the future while in Singapore. Over a Singapore Sling with a view of Marina Bay, we decided to fully focus on our studies and finish our degrees in the coming years. After that, we promised ourselves, we would return to the Philippines.

But until then, Germany came first – completing our studies was the next big goal. That moment – cocktail in hand, the sparkling lights of Marina Bay before us, and the warm night air around us – felt like a quiet agreement with the future. It was a sign that our second home would never truly let us go, even if Germany remained our base for now.

A special moment for the two of us – in front of Marina Bay in Singapore

Japan

After Andrew successfully completed his studies, we spontaneously planned a trip together – just the two of us. Our destination was Japan, and the trip was simply unforgettable. In Tokyo, we immersed ourselves in the vibrant diversity of the city, explored Akihabara, strolled through Ueno, and visited the famous Ghibli Museum. Our journey continued on to Yokohama and Mount Fuji before we took the train to the Kansai region to visit Kyoto and Osaka. The temples, shrines, and the dynamic energy of both cities deeply impressed us – even though our stay there was brief.

Back in Tokyo, we made a stop at the new Olympic Stadium, which was still under construction at the time in preparation for the 2020 Games. With a touch of melancholy – and even more anticipation – we promised ourselves that one day we'd return together to experience the city and the country again. The world is vast, and our sense of adventure had been awakened. But we also knew that real life was waiting – I was already working, and Andrew was about to begin his own career.

So, the next trip had to be carefully planned. We decided that after three years, it was time to return to the Philippines. Together with our parents – just like old times – we wanted to revisit our second home. In December 2018, the time had finally come: we flew to the Philippines for five weeks to spend time as a family in our mother's homeland.

An adventure that had taken us far into the world ultimately led us back to our roots.

* * *

The famous robot from the film *Laputa: Castle in the Sky* at the Ghibli Museum

Wearing a traditional yukata through Kyoto

Andrew in front of the iconic orange torii gates in Kyoto

* * *

Diving into the world of Pikachu & friends – Pokémon Store, Tokyo

Chapter 19: Christmas 2018

The four of us flew to the Philippines – this time over Christmas and New Year's, for the first time in 21 years. I still vividly remembered our last Christmas holiday there, especially the plastic Christmas tree with the melting chocolate ornaments.

Our journey began in Manila, a city we hadn't visited in many years. Parts of it had become impressively modern, and the neighborhoods lit up for the holidays were especially radiant. Christmas is celebrated with color and exuberance in the Philippines, and the festive spirit was felt everywhere.

Back in our home village, we were welcomed with countless warm encounters and joyful surprises. The family greeted us with a festive reception, and it felt as though we had never been away. Naturally, we returned to the underwater world as well – once again reminded of the breathtaking beauty of the Philippine coasts.

We celebrated New Year's Eve together with the family – a reunion filled with warmth and happiness to be back. The 2018 trip, with all its little moments and heartfelt reunions, remains one of our most treasured year-end experiences.

* * *

Christmas lights in Manila, 2018

Snowmen under palm trees – San Roque 2018

* * *

Our parents on the beach of San Roque

Diving trip in 2018

Christmas Celebration at the Children's Village

As so often during our trips to the Philippines, our journey once again led us to the children's village – a place we've visited time and again over the years. The children's village is a project by *Kinderhilfe Philippinen* and offers new hope and opportunities to many children who have experienced difficult circumstances from a very young age (more on this in Chapter 24).

Our visits have always been marked by heartfelt warmth, and the dedicated staff never fail to share new developments and moving stories. This time, we had the chance to witness something truly special: the Christmas celebration at the children's village.

As often happens when people come together with open hearts, it became a celebration full of warmth, joy, and a strong sense of togetherness. The event began with a generous meal – there was plenty of food and drink for everyone. The children had prepared dances and short performances with great dedication, which they proudly presented.

After the cultural portion, the event transformed into a cheerful little disco. The children danced with carefree energy – the atmosphere was lighthearted and filled with joy. For many of them, the children's village is not only a place of safety, but a true home – one that offers structure, security, and a renewed sense of belonging.

As the evening slowly drew to a close, the dancing and celebration carried on with enthusiasm. As always, we were warmly invited to join the next Christmas celebration – if we happened to be in the Philippines at that time again.

That evening was another powerful reminder of just how valuable the work at the children's village is – and how much light, joy, and solidarity it brings into the lives of the children and the wider community.

Dubai

On our return flight from the Philippines, we made a stopover in Dubai to visit our mum's cousin, who was working there with her husband. We took the opportunity to explore the city and enjoyed a few exciting days. But the real surprise came on our way back: when we tried to check in at the airport, we were asked to step aside for a moment. Our flight was overbooked, and we were offered a deal we simply couldn't refuse – fly one day later in exchange for a free flight voucher for each of us, plus an overnight stay in a five-star hotel, including breakfast, lunch, and dinner – all free of charge.

Thanks to the generous buffer we had built into our travel schedule, this was no problem at all. We gratefully accepted the offer and looked forward to an unexpected extra day in Dubai. The hotel was beautiful, and the next morning we were treated to a luxurious breakfast buffet – where we heard a particularly interesting story. The restaurant manager, a friendly woman from South Korea, told us that just a few days earlier, the K-pop band *Momoland* had stayed at the hotel. The Filipino staff had been thrilled and eagerly followed the group's movements, which sparked a fun conversation between us and the manager.

She told us about the upcoming Expo in Dubai and all the major construction projects still underway. She also spoke passionately about her home country, South Korea, and highly recommended that we visit one day. The idea stuck with us – and eventually inspired a trip we would take a few years later.

That extra day felt almost surreal, and when we were

picked up in a limousine and taken to the airport for check-in, the experience felt complete. We were already looking forward to our next trip, which we began planning while still at the hotel: at the same time next year, we would return to the Philippines – back to our second home. Again for Christmas and New Year's. And, of course, with the free flights now in hand, the planning was a whole lot easier.

Huey, Dewey, and Louie in the Miracle Garden, Dubai

Chapter 20: Dad

One afternoon, we were still a family – everything was fine. And yet, that very afternoon, everything changed. It happened suddenly and far too quickly, a moment that completely threw us off course. Just like that, we were no longer four, but three. Just like that, we felt a kind of loneliness that was hard to comprehend. The sudden emptiness that crept into our lives turned familiar places into painful reminders, and everyday things became strange. Our dad was no longer with us.

The weeks that followed were the hardest we had ever lived through. Every move, every step felt heavy – and yet somehow necessary. Life had to go on, but it all felt strangely hollow. The world kept turning, but we seemed to be moving alongside it, not within it.

The funeral became a reunion with many people we hadn't seen in years: friends, family, acquaintances – all came to say goodbye. And yet, that day felt surreal. It was as if we were watching ourselves from the outside, as if none of it could really be happening. The time that followed became a constant struggle with memories.

Over the years, the loss didn't get easier, but we learned to live with it. At some point, we realized we weren't alone in our grief. Many of our friends lost their own fathers in the years that followed – one after another. Our conversations changed: we were no longer just young adults, but people learning to cope with loss.

Time passes, and people fade away. We hold on to the memories as best we can – but even they change, grow fainter, and sometimes slip beyond our grasp. And so, there isn't much more we can write – except that we hope what remains is enough to keep him alive within us.

The Hohenfeld Mountain Church in September is a true place of peace and reflection. Here, you can find tranquility and leave everyday life behind.

Favorite Restaurant

There are places that stay with us over the years—not because they're particularly spectacular or tell a grand story, but simply because they've become part of our lives. Just like our favorite restaurant in Würzburg – a small Vietnamese place right in the heart of the city. A place we returned to again and again – sometimes as a family of four, sometimes just the three of us, and sometimes only two. It became a constant: a place where we were known and greeted, where we came together, shared a meal, and briefly escaped the rush of everyday life.

We no longer remember exactly when we first went there. It must have been around 2015, when we discovered it by chance. From then on, we went regularly – whenever we were in town, whenever we craved something familiar, or simply when we wanted good food. The owner and her family, originally from Vietnam, came to know us well. And every time we were there, there was a smile, a warm greeting, sometimes a short chat.

Then came the day when our dad was no longer with us. That first visit without him felt strange—almost surreal. When we placed our order, the owner asked, as she always did, "Is your dad not with you today?" We exchanged a glance, dodged the question, and simply replied, "Not today," letting the silence hang in the air. It was too fresh, too close, too heavy to talk about.

But the next visit came, and with it, the question again. This time, we had decided to tell her. After we finished eating, she looked at us again: "And your dad? Not with you today either?" We paused for a moment. "He passed away," we said quietly. She stopped, held her breath for a second. We paid, said goodbye—and then something happened that moves us to this day.

Before we left, she handed us 20 euros. "For flowers," she said softly.

After lunch, we went to a flower shop, bought a bouquet, and drove up to the church on Hohenfelder Hill. The grave still had no headstone, only a simple wooden cross. In the background lay the city, the Main River—and the train tracks, where an ICE sped toward Frankfurt Airport. The same train we would be taking just a few days later.

This time, there would only be three of us sitting at the table on the ICE. One seat would remain empty.

From Hohenfelder Hill, there's a wide view over

Kitzingen and the Main River, while an ICE train passes by, coming from the east, heading through Würzburg toward Frankfurt.

Chapter 21: Christmas 2019

Our last flight to the Philippines was different from all the ones before.

This time, it was just the three of us – Mum, Andrew, and me. On the plane, there were only three window seats left, no aisle seat available for Dad. So we sat close together, but his absence was unmistakable. The empty space next to us was deeply felt, and with every mile we got closer to our destination, the feeling of emptiness grew. It was a strange sensation – traveling to a familiar place, but no longer as the family we once were.

Even the train ride to the airport had left us reflective. Dad had always been a part of these trips, and although he was no longer with us, his presence felt almost tangible – as if he had just stepped away for a moment and would be right back. But the silence his empty seat left behind was a quiet reminder of a time that was gone forever.

When we finally arrived in the Philippines, the sense of loneliness deepened. Friends and family welcomed us with open arms, offering comfort and sharing in our grief. Stories were told, tears were shed, and condolences were expressed. For many, our dad had been a good friend – a part of the community, always ready for a conversation or a word of advice. Now that he was gone, it felt as though a piece of that community had also been lost. And yet, we were grateful to be among people who knew him, valued him, and missed him with us.

That flight – and that journey – marked the end of an era. It was a quiet but clear reminder that we had to accept a new reality without our dad. But his memory lived on – in the stories that were shared, in the memories we carried, and in the hearts of those who would never forget him.

2019 in San Roque – a sunset you never forget

Chapter 22: Daily Routine

When we returned to Germany in January 2020, our last trip still felt close – and yet, a new and unfamiliar reality lay ahead: the mountain of tasks that awaits when handling the estate of a loved one. No one truly prepares you for it.

It felt like an endless stream of responsibilities. We moved from one step to the next, almost mechanically – not because we wanted to, but because it had to be done. The death certificate had to be presented at various institutions, contracts had to be canceled or transferred, notary appointments scheduled, documents sorted – and again and again, the feeling that we were starting all over. It became part of our daily lives, our new routine. The process stretched on for nearly a year – but looking back, it was also a quiet way of coping with grief. Every task completed helped us deal with the pain, offered distraction, and brought structure to a time when everything felt unsteady.

But it wasn't just grief that defined those months – the pandemic suddenly hit with full force. It brought uncertainty, fear, and constant worry, not only here in Germany but also for our family in the Philippines. During the COVID era, we lost more loved ones. Phone calls and messages became part of our daily routine – often the only way to find out how people were doing over there. The pandemic tore wounds into our lives that we hadn't anticipated, and the physical distance made everything even harder.

Those months felt like the world had held its breath – and yet everything changed so quickly. Saying goodbye to our dad, the many small new beginnings, and arriving in a reality without him – much of it felt surreal, but somehow we made it through.

When the COVID restrictions finally eased, we began to travel again – just the three of us. We still had an unused flight voucher from our dad. It felt as if he had left us one final invitation. This journey began with a visit to the Expo in Dubai, continued on to Rome, and even took us to South Korea. It was unfamiliar, sometimes painful, to travel without him – and yet, it felt as if he was with us.

Together in Seoul, 2024

* * *

In the desert of Dubai, 2022

Since then, however, we haven't been back to the Philippines. But now, we're planning another trip – partly expecting that many things have changed, and quietly hoping that maybe some things have stayed the same.

Over time, our travel habits have changed too, and we're no longer always traveling as a group of three. Sometimes there are four or even five of us, and other times just two – our family is big, and it's still growing.

Chapter 23: Family Reunion

The term *Familiennachzug* (family reunification) is often a topic of controversy in Germany. Unfortunately, it's frequently associated with stereotypes: images of supposedly overcrowded households relying entirely on government support, or the notion that entire family clans are simply "brought over to Germany" without contributing. These clichés are widespread – yet in most cases, they're far from the truth.

Our story of family reunification looks very different. For us, it means solidarity, connection, and the opportunity to be close again – even after years of being separated by great distances.

In 2022, we had a very special visit: our cousin, who had emigrated to England with his family and now works as a nurse in a hospital there, came to visit us in Germany. The welcome was warm – and, as with almost all our guests, a trip to Neuschwanstein Castle was a must.

A photo from that trip, which I later posted on Instagram, triggered a chain of coincidences – and ultimately led me to meet my current girlfriend. From the very beginning, the chemistry between us was just right. Even though she lived in Delmenhorst in northern Germany and I lived in Hohenfeld in south Germany, we didn't let the distance discourage us. Thanks to the ICE and regional trains, the journey – as long as everything ran on time – took about four hours. And surprisingly, it worked out really well.

When she eventually moved in with us, our family home once again became a lively place for four. My girlfriend, a Russian German with a big and loving family, brought new energy and a warm spirit that deeply enriched our family life.

Another family member had already come to Germany from the Philippines a year earlier: our cousin settled in Berlin and found a job as a nurse – a profession that is in high demand in Germany. As is traditional in many Filipino families, she supports her father and brother, who still live in the Philippines, with her income.

Her move to Germany also made it possible for our uncle – who had never left the Philippines before – to visit us. For the first time, he was able to see the world beyond his home country. It was a beautiful family reunion that showed how strong our bonds remain, despite the geographical distance.

Family reunification, as we experience it, is so much more than a legal term or a political talking point. It's about bringing people together, bridging distances, and sharing cultures. Our family keeps growing – and life remains an adventure. Every day is a gift we cherish to the fullest.

PART 4: PRESENT

Chapter 24: Kinderhilfe Philippinen

In 2021, one year after our return, we learned that Jürgen Schneidt, the founder of Kinderhilfe Philippinen, had passed away. The news reached us through the organization's newsletter, accompanied by a heartfelt letter honoring his life's work and the lasting impact of his commitment.

Jürgen had built something truly remarkable, and that final letter reminded us once again how many lives he had touched and how much he had accomplished. It was a quiet yet meaningful farewell to someone who had dedicated himself tirelessly to helping others.

Through his work, Jürgen not only influenced us personally but also created a legacy that lives on in every project supported by Kinderhilfe Philippinen. His dedication, passion, and humanity will never be forgotten.

About Kinderhilfe

Kinderhilfe Philippinen e.V. is a privately run, volunteer-based initiative founded by employees of the German TV network ZDF. With the following contribution, we would like to give you an insight into the valuable work of the organization and show just how much dedication and heart the people involved put into their efforts.

A special thank you goes to Friedhelm Stoll and his team, who took the time to answer our questions.

Perhaps we can not only inform you but also inspire you to support the cause – for example, through a donation.

1. What is the mission of Kinderhilfe Philippinen, and what specific goals does the organization pursue in the Philippines?

Since 1986, our village on the Philippine island of Leyte has provided a safe home for around 70 babies, toddlers, and young people. The mission of Kinderhilfe Philippinen is to offer a permanent home in the children's village to abused, orphaned, or otherwise disadvantaged children, and to give them the opportunity for a self-determined future through access to education.

2. Could you introduce some of the key projects currently being carried out? How do these projects impact the lives of the children?

Kinderhilfe Philippinen also continuously organizes medical treatment for children in need who do not live in the village and whose parents are without financial means.

After individually assessing the family's situation, the necessary medical treatment is funded in hospitals in Maasin, Tacloban, or Cebu – including transportation, accommodation, meals, medication, and doctors' fees.

3. What are the biggest challenges that Kinderhilfe Philippinen faces in its work?

A decline in donations requires careful and moderate budgeting.
Rising wages and prices in the Philippines – especially for food and medical supplies – as well as increasing bureaucratic requirements are increasingly limiting Kinderhilfe's ability to operate effectively on the ground.

4. How do you ensure that donations are used effectively and that the support truly reaches those who need it most?

Kinderhilfe Philippinen does not maintain an expensive administrative structure.
Donations go directly to the children's village without any detours. The funds are used 100 percent for specific projects. For example: a donation of 20 euros can provide food for a child for an entire week.

5. Can you share examples of success stories where the organization's support has improved the lives of individual children or communities?

The four siblings Gilbert, Rey, Madelyn, and Reyesther Espejo came to the children's village as toddlers – the oldest, Gilbert, was six years old at the time. They lived there until completing their education.

Afterward, they moved into a house in Padre Burgos that had been made available by a German national who left the Philippines. The house was provided through Jürgen Schneidt. They lived there until each of them started their own families. Today, all four siblings are married and still live in Padre Burgos.

Gilbert is married to a former social worker from the children's village. After graduating as a teacher, he began working for the school authority at the Central School in Padre Burgos and also works part-time as a sports instructor at the village.

Rey works as an IT technician for the local police department and also teaches music part-time to the children at the village.

Madelyn is employed as a nurse at the local hospital, and Reyesther works as a secretary at the mayor's office in Padre Burgos.

These success stories clearly show how Kinderhilfe Philippinen prepares children for life in the community and actively supports their education and career development.

6. What are the future plans and visions of Kinderhilfe Philippinen e.V.? What projects or initiatives are you planning for the coming years?

In the past, Kinderhilfe Philippinen also supported the improvement of rural infrastructure around the children's village: playgrounds, kindergartens, schools, hospitals, and medical facilities were built – in total, more than 300 buildings.

Additionally, numerous manual water pumps were installed to supply rural areas with clean water, always with a focus on employing local workers.

A major long-term project remains the self-sustained

operation of the children's village.

The village is funded entirely by donations from Germany, which, unfortunately, have been steadily declining over the years.

For this reason, we have launched an initiative to involve Philippine authorities – such as the DSWD (Department of Social Welfare and Development), local municipalities, and the provincial government of Southern Leyte – in sharing the financial responsibility for maintaining the children's village.

7. What role do volunteers and donors play in your work, and how can interested individuals actively contribute or offer support?

Without ongoing (financial) donations, a long-term project like this would not be sustainable.

Without volunteer support, the administrative management would not be feasible or financially responsible.

8. How does the organization ensure that cultural and local specifics are taken into account in its project work?

The local board is made up entirely of Filipinas and Filipinos.

Projects are always evaluated locally for their relevance and cost-effectiveness.

Project and construction management is always handled by staff members of Kinderhilfe.

Local companies and workers are actively involved as partners.

There is close cooperation with the municipality of Padre Burgos.

Kinderhilfe is an integral part of the community and is

actively involved in cultural and humanitarian efforts.

9. How can donors be sure that their money is being used responsibly? Do you provide regular updates or reports?

- Transparent use of funds through access to budget plans and annual financial statements.
- Regular newsletters
- Homepage
- Impressions through video clips
- Facebook
- Special reports

10. What final message would you like to share with our readers? Why is their support so valuable?

We, Kinderhilfe Philippinen e.V., extend a helping hand to children. With a donation, anyone can play a part in giving children a future together with us. That has been our mission since 1986.

Donate

A donation of just 20 euros can help provide food for a child for an entire week. So donate – every euro counts!

Donations to:

KinderHilfe Philippinen e.V. Mainz

Rheinhessen Sparkasse

IBAN: DE64 5535 0010 0000 0002 40

SWIFT-BIC: MALADE51WOR

You can find additional information on the ZDF website via the link provided:

https://www.zdf.de/unternehmen/verantwortung/gemeinwohl/kinderhilfe-philippinnen-100.html

Chapter 25: Your Questions

We are often asked many – and often very similar – questions about our background: about our story, our experiences, and what it's really like to grow up between two cultures. In this chapter, we want to answer exactly those questions.

This time, we're splitting the answers between us, because even though we've experienced so much together, each of us looks back on the past from our own unique perspective.

Our memories, feelings, and thoughts don't always align – and that's exactly what makes our story so special.

Additional questions you might still have will be discussed together in our podcast *"Alman ist Lost"* – in the episode titled *"Im Jeepney durch die Zeit."*

And now: Here are your questions – and our very personal answers.

Questions for Christian

1. What does home mean to you personally?

Home is freedom. When I feel free, I feel at home – and that can be anywhere.

2. Is there a specific moment from your childhood that especially shaped your connection to the Philippines?

The school parade for the annual village fiesta was something truly special. Every year, it looked a little different – and yet, at its core, it always stayed the same. Each class showcased colorful costumes, dances, and loud music. These vibrant memories will stay with us forever.

3. What role do Filipino traditions play in your life today?

The regular gatherings with the Filipino community in Germany have meant a lot to me. It's part of the tradition to come together, share a meal – and at the end, take home leftovers, which often make up half the buffet.

 4. What memories of your family in the Philippines are especially important to you?

The last gathering of all my mum's siblings with our grandfather was something truly special. We took a group photo together – it would be the last time everyone was still alive. Moments like these must be cherished, because time is relentless.

* * *

5. Is there a Filipino dish that holds a special meaning for you?

In the Philippines, roast pig is called *Lechon*. The pigs are traditionally stuffed with spices and local vegetables, then slowly cooked over an open fire. They often come from the village's own livestock or from nearby farmers who have raised them over the years. When a special occasion like a birthday comes around, the whole family gathers – and *Lechon* is a must. It's simply part of our culture and celebrations.
Today, I'm a vegetarian – which means that at such events, I usually just enjoy the side dishes.

6. Is there a German dish that holds a special meaning for you?

Dumplings with gravy from our grandma – and potato salad from our dad.

7. If you had to describe the Philippines in one word, what would it be

Timelessness. After two days at the latest, I forget what day of the week it is. It's a feeling I really miss.

8. How would you compare the mentality of the people there with the German mentality?

Openness – you feel it right away. Doors are open, visitors are always welcome. When you walk through the streets, you encounter life: people, conversations, laughter.
In Germany, it's quite different. That doesn't have to be

negative – I also enjoy having time to myself. But for someone new to Germany, this reservedness can feel very strange at first.

9. Which values or principles from Filipino culture would you want to pass on to your own children?

Ease. A simple word, but it says a lot. Personally, I've always carried it with me. No matter the situation, you should approach it with a certain lightness. Everyone can do that. Of course, it's not always easy – but that's exactly why this trait is so valuable. After all, how else am I supposed to deal with people in a bad mood?

10. What do you think are the biggest misunderstandings or clichés about the Philippines that you often hear?

In Germany, many assume the Philippines is a "third-world country." While poverty is still widespread, the middle class is steadily growing, and the level of education is very high. Also, English is widely spoken, making it easy to get around. So: head to the Philippines – and be ready to be surprised!

11. Do you feel more German, more Filipino, or like a mix of both?

Actually, I simply feel German – but sometimes I have to mention my "migration background." It's a circumstance that feels somewhat strange in 2025. I'd also describe myself as a European with Filipino roots.

12. Have you ever thought about living permanently in the Philippines? Why or why not?

* * *

In the past, yes – I could imagine it quite well. But today, not so much anymore. By now, I've probably become too "German," and I really appreciate living in the heart of Europe. Still, one should never rule anything out completely. Maybe one day I'll be drawn to the Philippines for an extended stay after all.

Questions for Andrew

1. What does home mean to you personally?

A place that gives me security, peace, and a sense of belonging.

2. Is there a specific moment from your childhood that especially shaped your connection to the Philippines?

I became aware at an early age of how poverty is often simply accepted in society. I remember a moment from my childhood. We were eating at Jollibee, and outside the restaurant sat a homeless man. He looked old, worn down by life. I ordered extra food just so I could give him what I didn't finish. To me, it was clear: helping others should have no limits – neither age nor social status should ever stand in the way.

3. What role do Filipino traditions play in your life today?

Without a doubt: the food. Whenever you're invited by Filipino friends or relatives, traditional food is always at the center – rich, flavorful, and filled with memories. Along with it comes the warm atmosphere, the joy, and the sociable spirit of the people. That combination is simply one of a kind.

4. What memories of your family in the Philippines are especially important to you?

* * *

Sharing meals always held a special meaning – often four to five generations would sit together at the table for lunch or dinner. Sometimes it even took place on the beach – during low tide, with a pot of rice, plates, and cutlery. The seafood was freshly gathered and eaten together on the spot. They were simple, yet unforgettable moments.

5. Is there a Filipino dish that holds a special meaning for you?

Spring rolls – of course, because of their unique taste, but also because of the variety of recipes that have been passed down from generation to generation.

6. Is there a German dish that holds a special meaning for you?

Potatoes with fried egg and spinach – in the past, this was often served with Leberkäse, a typical Franconian-Bavarian dish. Today, as a vegetarian or pescatarian, I leave out the meat. This dish was my German grandmother's traditional meal and was served at least once a week. In our early childhood, we almost daily ate lunch together with three generations – a tradition that remains memorable to this day.

7. If you had to describe the Philippines in one word, what would it be?

Diversity.

8. How would you compare the mentality of the people there with the German mentality?

* * *

Every mentality has its strengths and weaknesses. A good example is punctuality. In Germany, it is taken for granted to stick to schedules – structure, reliability, and timeliness. In the Philippines, however, this often feels like a fight against windmills. What seems clearly regulated here quickly loses significance there.

For a German immersing themselves in this culture, learning to go with the "flow" is essential – and sometimes simply saying, "Well, that's just how it is." Fighting against windmills accomplishes little – in this case, patience and calmness are the better approach.

9. Which values or principles from Filipino culture would you want to pass on to your own children?

The ease with which problems are handled in the Philippines is remarkable. It's often seen as a matter of mentality – yet it is deeply shaped by culture. Challenges, conflicts, or minor misunderstandings are not blown out of proportion.

You won't suddenly find an angry neighbor around the corner because you parked wrong, played music too loud, or smoke from the grill drifted into a window. For many Filipinos, something only becomes a real problem when it can no longer be resolved with time. Everything has its own rhythm – and in the end, what matters is that everyone smiles together again.

10. What do you think are the biggest misunderstandings or clichés about the Philippines that you often hear?

It shows ignorance—and is primarily racist—when Filipinos are broadly labeled with offensive terms like "slit eyes." Such language is hurtful and has no place in respectful interaction.

Aside from sharing a maritime border, the Philippines has little cultural connection with China. The Filipino population is strongly influenced by the American education system. English is part of daily life: many children learn it as early as kindergarten, and most people speak it fluently.

Additionally, over two million Filipinos live and work abroad—they are part of a globally connected world. Anyone with little knowledge of Asian cultures should be careful not to make ignorant or sweeping generalizations. After all, Japanese, Koreans, Chinese, Taiwanese, Thai, Indonesians, and Filipinos differ culturally just as much as English and Greeks do.

11. Do you feel more German, more Filipino, or like a mix of both?

A 50/50 mix – I ate my schnitzel with rice.

12. Have you ever thought about living permanently in the Philippines? Why or why not?

Living permanently in the Philippines – no, I can't imagine that at the moment. But from the end of October to the end of March, I would love to be there. I just can't deal with the gray, gloomy weather in Germany during those months.

You almost automatically fall into an emotional low: you start your day in the dark and stop working in the dark again – without seeing a single ray of sunshine. That really gets me down every year anew.

Chapter 26: Podcast "Alman ist Lost"

We've always had countless ideas and plans swirling in our minds. Our experiences, thoughts, and observations constantly generate a wide range of ideas – often completely unrelated to one another.

From a series about the everyday life of a small football club in a German village, to a science fiction novel exploring the arrival of aliens and the mystery of the Fermi Paradox – anything is possible when we're involved.

To organize and share these thoughts, we launched our podcast *"Alman ist Lost"* in 2022. The term *"Alman"* is often used to playfully poke fun at stereotypical German behavior. Originally a Turkish word simply meaning *"German,"* today it's more of a lighthearted nod – used, for example, when someone is overly punctual, strictly follows rules, or insists on bringing their own folding chair when camping. It's not meant to offend – rather, it's a humorous wink at habits many Germans are known for.

Our podcast, however, covers much more than the name might suggest – we talk about everything that moves us: political, social, and deeply personal topics.

The subjects range from constitutional debates about banning the AfD to philosophical reflections on extraterrestrial life and the state of our world.

But for us, the podcast is more than just a space for conversation.

It's our way of processing experiences and staying connected as brothers – even when life takes us to different places.

In both our personal and professional lives, we're sometimes far apart – occasionally even on different continents.

It's quite likely that the podcast's name will change over time – from *"Alman ist Lost"* to something that better reflects what it has grown into.
What will definitely remain, though, is the continuous numbering of our episodes.

This steady structure provides us not only with orientation but also with a sense of consistency – almost like a small piece of eternity.

As someone who loves numbers and precise calculations, I came up with a little future scenario:

Our first episode aired on May 10, 2022 – that's our fixed starting point.
If we continue releasing episodes every Tuesday without a break, we would reach:

- Episode 1000 on July 2, 2041
- Episode 2000 on August 31, 2060

And our big dream?

That we'll still be podcasting together in the year 2100.
If everything continues as planned, episode 4053 would be released on January 5, 2100.

We'd be 107 and 105 years old by then – and honestly, that idea has something magical about it.

Two old brothers who just never stopped talking to each other.
And the topics? We'll never run out.

PART 5: FUTURE

Chapter 27: Democracy

We worry about our future – about the direction in which our society is heading.

In times of climate change, the future is no longer something we can take for granted. Countries like the Philippines, with their thousands of islands and millions of people living in coastal areas, are already among the most vulnerable regions in the world. The climate crisis is a reality – and it shows us once again how closely political, social, and ecological issues are intertwined.

That is precisely why we have decided to get even more involved. Looking the other way is no longer an option.

After the results of the 2025 federal election, we made up our minds: we would join the SPD (Social Democratic Party of Germany). The fact that the AfD – which calls itself the "Alternative for Germany" – received 20% of the vote deeply shocked us. A party that denies man-made climate change and holds positions where human dignity seemingly no longer matters is gaining massive influence. And this in a country whose constitution begins with the words:

"Human dignity shall be inviolable." (Article 1 of the Constitution or *Grundgesetz*)

This development shakes us to the core. We cannot and will not simply accept it.

Instead of just watching, we have decided to actively stand up against it.

At the same time, we observe with concern in our immediate surroundings that positions far removed from our Constitution and its core values are becoming increasingly socially acceptable and perceived as "normal." This shift in what can be said and thought affects us deeply – and strengthens our resolve to actively counteract it.

Those who know us – or have gotten to know us through reading this book – know that certain values are especially close to our hearts: social justice, democratic action, and respectful interaction with one another.

Our decision to join the SPD is not only shaped by the current political situation but also by our family history. Our grandfather, born in 1923, was himself a member of the SPD. From stories, we know about brothers of our grandfather and other family members who were also politically active at the time. Unfortunately, we have not yet been able to fully reconstruct our family history. We heard about an uncle of our grandfather who had to flee to Switzerland, and our family name appears several times on the war memorial in our village.

These traces make us curious, and we will continue researching.

Our concern is not only for the future – but also for democracy.
For us, it is the most important and best form of government we have.

A look at both German and Philippine history clearly shows the depths to which authoritarian systems can lead. Minorities usually suffer the most under such conditions – they need democracy more than anyone else. And we count ourselves as part of such a minority. We are Germans with a migration background – or, as we sometimes jokingly say, *"foreigners with a migration background."*

We know both perspectives, move between cultures, and repeatedly experience how quickly people are put into boxes.

All the more important for us is that democratic values are not only protected but also actively lived.

One issue that is especially close to our hearts is social justice – and in countries like the Philippines, this term takes on an especially urgent meaning. There, the rich and poor live side by side – yet in completely different worlds. This inequality is visible every day, tangible, and painful.

That's why we also make an appeal to our readers: Support Kinderhilfe Philippinen – every contribution helps create opportunities where there otherwise would be none.

But even in Germany, the gap between rich and poor is growing. We observe this development with great concern. If we do not firmly oppose it, it will continue to divide our society – until it is eventually too late.

Social justice is not a luxury – it is a prerequisite for a functioning democracy.

Democracy thrives on participation.

We want to do our part – for a fairer, more humane, and sustainable society.

Chapter 28: The Year 2100

It is January 5, 2100. Tuesday. 1:00 PM.
Episode 4053.
We sit side by side, just like so many times before. It is one of those clear January days when the air almost smells like a new beginning.
We are 107 and 105 years old.

And yes – we're still here. Not as fast as before, perhaps a bit slower in movement, but sharp in mind, calm in heart, and still full of curiosity. And above all: together.
We nod to each other. Briefly, without words. Then we hit "record."
"Welcome to episode 4053 of our podcast…"
Our voices fill the room. Not quite as clear as before, maybe a little rougher – but full of warmth and life. It has become a ritual that connects us. For decades. And even today, in this new century, we sit here as always. Together.

And we talk.

Our first topic today: trips to Mars.
What was once a thing of the future has long become everyday reality. We talk about the first missions, the setbacks, the excitement – and how an idea became reality. Today, people regularly fly to Mars. There are colonies – not as places to escape to, but as an expansion of our possibilities. Earth remains our home. Yet the horizon has

broadened. Space is no longer distant – and the sense of wonder has never faded.

Our second topic moves us deeply: the last weapons displayed in the Museum of Modern History.
We speak in hushed tones, almost reverently. About a world that has learned that violence is not the answer. That war is no longer necessary. The last conflicts are decades behind us. Today, children grow up in peace – in a world without armies, without frontlines, without defense budgets. Our greatest human achievement: peace.

Our third topic: Fake news – and the lessons we have learned from it.
We recall how people in the 2010s and 2020s voted based on false assumptions. How algorithms, targeted disinformation, and emotional manipulation helped crazy presidents come to power – leaders who divided rather than united. It was a dangerous time when facts lost their importance and truth seemed negotiable.

But we also talk about what has changed. Today, the handling of information is clearly regulated by law. Digital platforms bear responsibility. Education systems teach media literacy. And above all: independent science is once again at the center of societal decisions. Not opinions, but findings. Not power games, but responsibility. A foundation on which trust could be rebuilt – piece by piece.

Now we come to a topic that has always been important to us: basic income.
We talk about how it was introduced worldwide and how it has changed the world. No one lives in fear of survival anymore. Food, housing, medical care, and access to education have become a given for everyone.

Poverty? A term from the past – everywhere in the world. The global basic income hasn't solved all problems, but it has laid the foundation for a fairer, more humane society. A world where solidarity and participation no longer depend on origin or wealth. It's not a perfect system – but it was a new beginning. And it worked.

And then we talk about our planned trip to the Philippines.
The effects of climate change – they are not forgotten, but they have been overcome. The Philippines have recovered. The islands, the sea, the people – they have become part of a new paradise. We talk about reforestation, new coastlines, cities that are now green instead of gray. And we look forward: to our family there, to the reunion, to arriving home.

Another item on our agenda: the Jeepney Museum.
The old, brightly painted vehicles – once symbols of the chaos and beauty of everyday life – are now lovingly restored and on display. We imagine ourselves standing in front of them, smiling, taking photos, sharing stories. About our roots. About what remains.

In between, we laugh. Share anecdotes. Toss the ball back and forth like we always have. We drift off, then come back again. And yet we both feel: this episode is more than just another Tuesday. It's a celebration of what is possible – and a thank you for all the years, all the conversations, all those who have walked with us.
And at some point, while the recording is still going, I look out the window. The sky is blue. I think back to the day we wrote this text:
We sat by the window, went over the text one last time together, looked up at the sky – and felt the excitement for what lay ahead.

Afterword

As brothers, both engaged in our respective professions and working on various projects, we rarely find time to pause. Our minds are full of ideas, plans, and commitments – yet our own childhood has never truly left us.

Writing this book was a journey – not only into the past, but also into ourselves. It felt like time travel, guiding us through the defining moments of our lives.

The inspiration for this book came when we learned that the *Frankfurter Buchmesse 2025* would feature the Philippines as the guest country. After a bit of research, we realized there is hardly any literature that reflects stories like ours – about people whose identity is anchored between two worlds. Yet we know many share a similar story.

It's not just about the Philippines. It's about all those who spent childhood summers in the homeland of one parent – about the richness of growing up between cultures, and the challenges and joys that come with that heritage.

Writing this book felt like opening an old photo album. It brought back memories that seemed long faded, and showed us how vivid that past still is.

It was a journey that reminded us how strong our roots are – even if they lie in two different cultures.

Of course, we wonder if there will be a follow-up book. We certainly have enough ideas and stories.

Maybe our next journey will take us through the kitchen – because food connects our two cultures just as much as our memories do.

We've often talked about writing a cookbook that reflects this very mix: "Schnitzel with Rice" – a culinary journey through our German-Filipino world.

Will it happen? Who knows. But the idea is there – and those who know us know: once we have an idea, it rarely lets go of us.

Over the years, many things have changed – but one thing has always stayed the same: the Jeepney.

Maybe today there are Bluetooth speakers instead of old cassette decks – but the spirit of the Jeepney remains unchanged.

It's loud, colorful, sometimes chaotic – but always alive. The Jeepney is part of the Philippines. A symbol of movement, community, and the feeling that everyone is on their way somewhere.

And that's exactly why we're so grateful you joined us on our Jeepney journey – and took this ride with us.

Whether you shared memories with us, saw yourselves in our stories, or simply got a small glimpse into our world – you were part of this ride.

The journey continues. And we're sure that our dad, with his world receiver, has long found the right frequency – and is listening to us.

In our vivid memories, he's right there with us: laughing, marveling, and full of joy at how time has changed.

Acknowledgements

In closing, we want to thank everyone who has accompanied and supported us on this journey. This book has been more than just a retrospective for us – it has been a journey to our roots, an opportunity to organize our memories and share them with others.

A special thanks goes to Jasmin, who tirelessly proofread our texts and lovingly reminded us – time and again – that it was time to finally publish. We know perfection doesn't exist, but sometimes you need someone who gently yet firmly pushes you toward the finish line. Thank you, Jasmin!

Our thanks also go to our mum, whose remarkable memory helped us bring many small and big details back to life.

A heartfelt thank you also goes to Helga: thanks to the video recorder she lent us, we were able to digitize old recordings and take an additional journey through time that inspired and moved us deeply.

Another big thank-you goes to Friedhelm Stoll and his team, who introduced us to the organization *Kinderhilfe Philippinen e.V.*.

Thank you to our family as well as our friends – for your support, your stories, and your belief in us. You have not only inspired us but also laid the foundation for much of what has found a place in this book. Thank you, too, for your honest feedback, ideas, and thoughtful input. Without you, this book would not be what it is today.

And finally: thank you to all of you who have read this book. Perhaps you recognized yourself in some of these moments. Perhaps you discovered new perspectives. In any case, we hope you were able to share a part of this journey with us.

Salamat, Danke and Thank you.

Christian und Andrew Weichselfelder
2025